A Paratrooper Remembers

Glen C. Drake

Waubesa Press
An imprint of Badger Books Inc.

© Copyright 2003 by Glen C. Drake
Published by Waubesa Press, an imprint of Badger Books Inc.
Cover photo of Glen C. Drake taken in France after the D-Day invasion.
Printed by LightningSource of Lavergne, Tenn.

ISBN 1-878569-92-9

Badger Books Inc.
P.O. 192, Oregon, WI 53575
Toll-free phone: (800) 928-2372
Web site: http://www.badgerbooks.com
E-Mail: books@badgerbooks.com
E-Mail: books@badgerbooks.com

This book is dedicated to Carla Jean, who urged me to write about my memories of World War II.

A special thank you to Pastor Steve Ohrtman of St. Paul's Lutheran Church, who made this book possible through his encouragement and determination to see my story in print.

Prologue

Carla,

When I was discharged from the service in December 1945, I was fed to the gills and there were two things I wanted to do. The first was to be with Char and the second was to forget the goddamned war. The first was easy, but the second took more doing. I finally realized that I would never be able to forget the war.

When we were in Liege, Belgium, the Krauts were sending in a buzz bomb every fifteen minutes on the minute. We could see them and hear them, and they were slow enough that a fighter plane could shoot them down. We knew that when the motor quit, it was coming down.

When we moved from Madison to Baraboo in 1953, I was still having a bad dream once in a while. One night I was fighting one of those Kraut pigs and when Mom managed to awaken me, I was in the process of choking her to death. She coughed and gasped for a few minutes before she could talk and tell me what happened. That really scared me, and that was when we went to twin beds.

The Krauts were still sending in their buzz bombs in 1953. One day I was standing on the sidewalk in front of Colby's store in my home town, Loyal, when one of the buzz bombs came in right over Joe Wedl's tavern. The motor stopped and I knew it was coming down so I hit the dirt and "Boom" I woke up. I had whacked the bridge of my nose on the edge of the night table and I had a big nose and two black eyes for a week.

Gradually through the years the war began to seem more like history than reality. Instead of trying to forget it all, I began bringing back memories. I know now I had been doing this all the while. I know now that no matter how much it hurt to have so many of my good friends and buddies killed, I can never forget them, and I know now I will never forget them.

There are still a few of my old buddies hanging in there, like Don Jakeway in Ohio. He is one of the few of us who went all the way and has been gathering material to write a book on the 508th. He asked me to send him a few of my memories and experiences. You have a copy of the stuff Carla typed for me to send to him.

Most of it will be on these tapes I am making for you, but there will be a few more items I hope you will enjoy.

— Dad

1

When we became actively involved in WW II and the draft started, I was on the farm with my grandparents, Frank and Nellie Catlin. Nellie was my Grandmother and Frank was my step-grandfather. There are quite a few photos of them in my old family album.

I loved them and I loved the farm. As far back as I can remember when I was a kid in school, I spent the entire summer vacation on the farm. The country roads then were dirt road, so you can believe the wild strawberries I picked along the ditch were dusty. They were dirty and they were tiny, but they sure had a big sweet and delicious flavor.

About a mile and a half east there was a small creek. I used to take a can of worms, a three-gallon pail, and an old cane pole that Grandpa cut down for me and go fishing. I would carry that pail full of water and fish home, and when Grandma fried them for us, those shiners and suckers and redhorse were as tasty as trout!

When I was old enough to drive the horses on the hay wagon, they paid me a nickel a load. What a deal!!!

Grandpa had eighty acres a mile north of the farm. It was about half woods. The other half had a little high ground with some good pasture but was mostly lowland, with a creek and some marsh grass and swamp hay. It wasn't really what would be considered a prime piece of land, but it was excellent feed for the cattle during the hot and dry summer months.

Every afternoon it was my job to go and bring the cows home for milking. We kept them overnight and in the morning, after they were milked, I would herd them back to the eighty.

There was a woods on the west side of the road and one afternoon while I was bringing the cows home, I looked into the woods and saw a big black bear. Grandpa had told me many times that I should never run the cows when I was bringing them home for milking because if they got excited they wouldn't let down their milk like they should. I don't remember for sure, but I suspect I may have pushed them a little after I saw that bear. Anyway, the next morning Grandpa and a couple of the neighbors, Fred and Louis Seefeldt, went out and converted that bear into steaks and roasts.

But to get back to the farm when WW II came along, our world was very small then, made up mostly of our families, our friends and neighbors, our radio, and the weekly newspaper.

We knew about Hitler and the trouble he had been raising in Europe because of the news reports on the radio. We would listen to him scream and rant and rave on the radio, but we didn't worry about him. Why should we? After all, he was just another maniac, and he was half a world away. And even after the yellow-bellied Japs attacked Pearl Harbor, it was a while before many of us knew how the war would affect us, because Japan was half a world away too.

Grandpa had two farms. He and Grandma and I were on one farm and there was a hired man and his wife on the other farm. It was a good life. I worked like a horse, ate like a horse, had muscles like a horse and I loved it. I should say I loved most of it, because there were a couple of things I didn't like.

Every Saturday afternoon we went into town to buy groceries. Grandpa and I always put on our dress shoes and a clean pair of overalls. Just because we were farmers didn't mean we had to smell like a barn. We went home to feed and milk the cows and then it was Saturday night. That may not sound exciting to you, but I can tell you that Saturday night was when Grandpa and I went out to do some howling.

About 3 ½ miles from our farm was the small village of Riplinger, population probably somewhere around 110 if you counted all the dogs. There was a feed mill where we took our oats and corn to have it ground for feed. There was a box factory where the logs we hauled during the winter were made into cheese boxes and berry boxes. There was a filling station and a grocery store. And there was the big tavern and dance hall. Every Saturday night there was a dance — a wedding dance or a birthday dance, or maybe just a plain dance — and that was where Grandpa and I did our thing. The band was whoever they could get, usually a concertina player, a fiddler, and a guitar with harmonica. Doesn't sound like much, but they sure did make good music! At least it was good after a couple of whiskey and cokes. We always had a few drinks, but we didn't hang one on — we were too busy dancing and having fun. We usually got home a little after 1 A.M., and even though it was Sunday we still got up at 4:15 A.M. because the cows had to be milked every morning and every night at the same time.

2

By now you're probably wondering what all this has to do with my memories of the war. Frank and Nellie were more like my father and mother than my parents were, and I can never think about the war without remembering I had to leave them and the farm.

My brother, Verland, had enlisted in the Air Corps and was in training camp in Texas. I tried to enlist in the Air Corps, thinking wouldn't it be fun if we could fly together? There was never a hog sent to market in more prime condition than I was, but when they saw my application and learned I had dental plates, they turned me down without even calling me in for a physical exam. That kinda pissed me off a little, and I thought O.K., fight your damn war without me. I didn't tell them this, but I sure could think it, because as a farmer I had an automatic exemption from the draft. If I didn't enlist or volunteer, there was no way they could get me, and I decided they could do their thing without me.

The radio was a big part of our small world, and was probably seventy-five perent of our entertainment. A few of our favorite programs were Fred Allen, Jack Benny and Rochester, Fibber McGee and Molly, Burns and Allen, and Ed Wynn. As I think back now, it is amazing how they seemed to be right there with us.

I will get to some of my memories of the war, but first I have to keep you on the farm with me for a while, because I was there when Mom and I had our first date.

Mom was teaching in Loyal, and was sharing a rented bedroom with another teacher, Jean Krash. One of the kids I grew up with through grade school and high school was Neil Oestreich.

One day Neil called me and said he had been trying to get a date with Jean, but she wouldn't go out with him unless it would be a double date with Char, and would I date Char. Neil was a good friend, but I told him no way. I hadn't met Char, but I knew who she was — a blonde schoolteacher, and I didn't go for blondes or schoolteachers.

A few days later Neil came out to the farm and he finally talked me into it. I still didn't care too much for it, but Neil said he had already talked with the girls and they had agreed to go out with us the next Saturday night.

And so, it was the night of September 5, 1942, when Mom and I had our first date. We decided to go to Club 10. It was called Club 10 because it was on Hwy 10, out in the boondocks between Marshfield and Neilsville. It wasn't a plush place, but was very popular because it had a reputation for serving good food.

In those days dancing was permitted in the taverns and no matter where you went there was a jukebox. It was a nickel a song, which was probably why many called it the nickelodeon. If business was good, many times the bartender would push a button on the back of the machine and it would keep playing.

Beer was five cents a glass and ten cents a mug. Booze was ten cents a shot for the cheap stuff and fifteen cents a shot if you went to the top shelf. If you had a booth in the back room you danced there, but if the booths were full and you had to sit at the bar, there was no problem — you danced in the bar room.

Most of the taverns in town closed at 1 A.M., but those out in the country could stay open as long as there was any business. We ate and drank and danced the night away, and it was 5:30 A.M. when I got back to the farm. Somehow everything was go, and it wasn't long before Mom and I were dating almost every night. There weren't any more nights as long as that first one because we both had work to do. But we never hung it up until we had listened to our favorite radio program, "Moon River," at midnight. It was a program especially for boys and girls who like the lovey-dovey sentimental songs.

Everything seemed to be going fine, until the night Mom said she would never marry a farmer. She had been born and raised on a farm and now that she knew what life in town was like, there was no way she was going back. I knew that if I left the farm I would be cannon fodder. I didn't care about being in the Army and I didn't want to leave the farm and I didn't want to call it quits with Char. It seemed like no matter which way I turned I would be butting my head up against a brick wall, but still I had to make a choice. It is of no consequence now because it is history, but I have thought about it many times, and I have often wondered — could I have talked Mom into marrying a farmer?

I made my choice and gave up my exemption from the draft. A few days later I went with a busload of other draftees to the Induction Center in Milwaukee.

That was where they gave the physical exams to see if you were fit for service. The dentist checked all of my upper teeth and then started on the lower teeth. I couldn't believe it and I just had to tell him I had full dentures. What those physical exams amounted to was a farce — if you were blind, you were out; if you were cold you were dead and if you were warm you were in.

We were told that we were to report in at the reception center, which was Fort Sheridan, on December 21, 1942, but later they delayed it until December 28.

At that time, Auntie Gladys and Uncle Jack were living in Minneapolis, and it must have been during Thanksgiving vacation when Mom and I drove up to see them. We did go to see them, but the main reason we went was because we were going to be married. We both knew that was what we wanted, even though we had been dating for only a couple of months. I can't remember the reasons for changing our minds, but we decided to wait until the war was over.

My great-grandpa Albert Darton was born December 5, 1844, so when I last saw him on December 28, 1942, he was 98 years old. Grandpa sold his farm and we all moved into the big house in Loyal — he and Great-Grandma and my folks and me. It was a big five-bedroom house, and he paid $1,200 for it. It sounds cheap, but that was a hell of a lot of money in those days.

I had to say good-bye to him in his bedroom, because he hadn't been up and about for several days. He had told my mother he felt fine but was a little tired — he would stay in bed and rest a little and get up in the morning. He passed away a couple of days after I left, but I didn't know about it until a month or so later when my mail finally caught up with me.

Grandpa was a great guy, and he and I were good buddies all through the years. I didn't realize then, but I know now how fortunate I was. After all, how many kids can have their great-grandfather as a pal for over twenty years?

My mother said this was the first time she could remember Grandpa being sick in bed for a day. And he really wasn't sick then, because as he said, he felt good, was just a little tired.

3

I left home on a bus loaded with other draftees and went to the reception center at Fort Sheridan, where I spend a few days getting my Army issue of clothing, getting my shots, and writing some tests. I did quite well on what they called the mechanical aptitude test, so they shipped me to the Aberdeen Proving Grounds, where I was to spend six months in the ordinance school learning how to repair weapons.

However, before I could be accepted into the ordinance school, I had to have four weeks of basic training. After all, we were at war, and it was absolutely essential that each and every one of us be well trained on the fundamental basics necessary for being a good soldier. It was then I learned:

1. How to salute an officer;

2. How to march in a straight line;

3. How to do an "about face;"

4. How to be sure that the middle of my belt buckle was perfectly in a line with the row of buttons down my shirt front;

5. How to make the right folds for the blanket on my cot;

6. Also, believer it or not, they taught me how to shoot and clean a rifle.

The captain who was our company commander was a perfect example of obesity. He had the fat face and jowls of a hog ready for market, with an ass and a gut to match. His favorite past time was a court martial for someone in the company. We all hated his guts, just as all of the officers under him.

Every night some of us were chosen for guard duty. There were ten general orders we had to memorize word for word, and there was nothing wrong with that, and most of us could recite them backward and forward. But when you were on guard duty and all of a sudden, at 3 A.M., the captain came out inspecting the guard and said, "Soldier, what is your sixth general order?" and if you didn't recite it right then word for word you were in a court martial, which meant jail. Another of his favorite tricks was to grab and take your rifle — if he got it, you were a goner.

One of my favorite memories is the night McGregor was on guard duty. His post was to cover the front of a big warehouse located to hell and gone out in the boondocks. Mac was a big rough and tough Irishman. He was walking his post sometime during the night when all of a sudden this guy comes out of the dark and grabs for his rifle. Mac had heard a vehicle stop down the road a ways. He had no idea who it was, but he was on the alert, and when this guy came at him out of the dark, he did his duty and beat they guy to a pulp. When the ambulance arrived and there were some lights, Mac saw it was the captain. It had to be, because there was no one else to pull such crap. There was a hearing, of course, because there had to be a hearing when a private beat up a captain. It lasted long enough for Mac to testify how this guy jumped him in the dark, and "Nobody takes my rifle away from me when I am on guard duty!" That was the end of it and we never saw the captain again.

January in Maryland was chilly and wet, just plan nasty, and we were outside most of the time. We had been told that if for any reason we did not complete the four weeks of basic training in one session, we would start over again.

One day our assignment was to march through the snow (and the mud) with full field packs for ten miles. Then we would pitch our pup tents for an overnight bivouac, and return to camp the next day. This would have been a breeze if I hadn't come down with a bad cold. I shouldn't have started it, but there was no way in hell I was going to start another four weeks of basic. I did not know when the ambulance came to get me during the night in bivouac. I went to sleep in my tent and woke up in the hospital. During the next five days, I went from about 166 lbs to 144 lbs.

When I got out of the hospital, I expected to go back to start another four weeks of basic training, but for some reason they sent me to the Ordinance School.

We were trained in the maintenance and repair of small arms, which included everything from the 45-caliber pistol to the 20 mm cannon (which ain't too small).

Classes were a real grind. Five days a week we went from 8 A.M. to 5 P.M. The other two days we went from 8 A.M. to 9 P.M. I shouldn't say it was a grind because it really wasn't. For me it was fun, even though they poured it on us. Fun, I guess, because the harder they made it the more I learned and the easier it was.

We had written exams and practical exams (working on weapons). They would give us a 30-caliber machine gun or an M1 Garand rifle and say, "This thing ain't working like it should — fix it." That wasn't a problem, because there was only about so much they could foul up. The real headache came when we went to a table with one pile of pieces, and they said, "O.K. you guys, Drake will assemble the Thompson sub machine gun, Larson will assemble the M1 rifle and James will assemble the B.A.R." There was no problem until they blindfolded us and said, "Go!"

One day about noon we were told that classes were dismissed. This couldn't happen unless there was something important coming up. There was a company formation at 1 P.M. and we had to go out and watch a bunch of stupid paratroopers strut around in front of us. They sure did look sharp, with their uniforms that fit like a glove, their wings, and their shiny boots. They were sticking out their chests like each one of them thought he was the only rooster in the barnyard.

They were there to tell us we should volunteer to be paratroopers — we should jump out of a plane. Up until that day those guys were there, I didn't even know there was such a thing as a paratrooper. I had never been up in a plane and I didn't plan on going up in a plane. When they told me I had to go out and pitch a tent and sleep in the snow, I went out and pitched a tent and slept in the snow. And if they had told me I had to go up in a plane, of course, I would have gone up in a plane. But there was no way I was going to jump out of a plane unless it was on the ground.

So while I listened to those guys trying to recruit volunteers, I was thinking what a waste of time. Even when they mentioned the extra $50 a month jump pay, it didn't appeal to me.

One of those fellows in my class was a Negro. We sat together whenever we could and got to be good friends. He and I had the top grades all through the training course.

Then I received a letter from Mom, telling me we weren't going to wait any longer. She was coming to see me during Easter vacation and we'd be married. She sent me enough money to take a cab into town and pay for the marriage license. Good thing she did, because after deductions for laundry, insurance, a bond a month, etc. I had about $6.20 a month left on payday. That I had to use for cigarettes, candy bars, shoe polish and razor blades. There wasn't much left over, but I didn't need much.

They came on the train, my mother and your mother. I had made all the arrangements with our chaplain, and we were married in the chapel on the post. Needless to say, there was no honeymoon.

Classes continued and then one day I was told to report to the company commander in the orderly room. He told me that because of my high grades I could be an instructor in the ordinance school and would I be interested? After six months in the classroom, I thought it was about enough, and I told him I would rather be shipped out to a regular outfit.

A couple of weeks later we finished the course. We were all confined to the area and every day there was a list of those shipping out. Then I was told to report again to the company commander. This time he told me to pack my belongings and check into barracks #21. That upset me because I knew that was the building where all of the instructors were housed.

The captain remembered what I had told him before. He said he had tried to put in a word for me, but the orders had come through and there was nothing he could do.

When I told him I would transfer before I would be an instructor, he said that would be hard to do because the Ordinance had high priority — the only way to go was either to the air corps or the paratroopers. The air corps would have been my choice but I had tried to enlist there and had been turned down because of my dental plates.

I have fouled up now and then along the way, but that day in the orderly room when I lost my cool — that was probably one of the biggest mistakes I ever made. I say probably because after all, I did survive. But you can bet your buns, I sure as hell wouldn't do it again. If I had known then what I learned later, I would have packed my duffel bag and moved into barracks #21. With the high priority the ordinance had, I probably could have sweated out the war right there in the Aberdeen Proving Ground in Maryland.

Of course, knowing what I know now, I would have done the same thing. When the paratroopers were in our area recruiting volunteers, they left some application blanks in the orderly room. I asked the captain to give me one of them, filled it in, and went to the hospital for a physical exam. There were no problems, and one week later I was in Fort Benning, Georgia, and jump school. I think my first memory of Fort Benning is that the temperature was hotter than a four-balled tomcat.

I was not exactly in prime physical condition. In

fact, after my bout with pneumonia, and then sitting on my butt in ordinance school for six months, I was about as hard as soft butter. During the next couple of years the army and the war would show me a few examples of what hell on earth is like, and the first week in jump school was a prime example.

It was eight hours a day of calisthenics — exercises, judo and double time, Ho!! Run! Run! Run! All this was a little rough because Fort Benning was sand and sun and hot!

Even though the first day was rough, I think it was the easiest day of the week. It began with an orientation talk by the officer in charge of the jump school. He told us what we would be doing during each of the 4 weeks it would take us to qualify as a paratrooper. It was going to be tough, he said, which was a gross understatement, and then he wished us luck and hoped we would all earn our wings. Before he left he introduced the officer in charge of our class.

That guy was something else! The first thing he said was, "By God, I'm happy today. It looks like they finally sent me some men I can work with." He got off to a good start, but from then on, he sure didn't sound or act very happy. He strutted around in front of the class waving his arms around like he was a wound up robot. His voice was loud and raspy and it came out of the side of his mouth like a sneer or a snarl. We could all see right away he was really tough! It was, "By God" this and "By God" that, and damn and cuss and we knew that here was a real man.

"How do you like the boots you are wearing? Pretty damn nice, huh? Well, by God, they ain't yours yet. So you think you want to be paratroopers, huh? Well, by God, you came to the right place, and I sure as hell hope I can make paratroopers out of you guys. I keep hoping for a class that will graduate more than 50 percent. I really want that, but by God, I'll tell you right now, there ain't no gutless bastard going to get his wings."

He finally quit ranting and raving and introduced the sergeants that would be in charge of the class. Those guys were really something else. They were as loudmouthed and arrogant and overbearing as the officer, but they had something going for them. When it came to physical fitness, they were the cream of the crop, the best.

Then, on the first day of the first week, we got down to the business at hand — calisthenics. When class was dismissed, we went Double time! Ho! run back to the barracks. We had time to shower before going to the mess hall for supper chow. I was so pooped I wasn't hungry, but I went to eat anyway. The smell of the kitchen was too much — I just couldn't stomach the thought of food. I went back to the barracks and crawled into my bunk.

The barracks were two stories, with double bunks up and down and I am still grateful I had a bottom bunk, even though it was on the second floor. They woke us at 5 A.M. I was going to get up but I couldn't make it. I was so stiff and sore I couldn't even lift my head. It had to be done. So I worked my way to the edge of the bunk, then rolled off and landed on the floor on my hands and knees. Then I grabbed the bunk post and pulled myself up to finally stand on my feet.

And so began the second day of the first week in jump school. At 5 A.M. it was hot, and it gradually warmed up as the day went on. It was another day of calisthenics, judo, and double time Ho! Run, Run, Run!

I am sure that every one of the guys who volunteered for jump school at Ft. Benning wanted to be a paratrooper. And I am sure they all tried to hang in there. But on the second day there were already some dropouts, and it wasn't simply because they were quitters. There were some who gave their best, but were just not physically capable.

The physical strain was great, but there was also a lot of mental stress. The sergeants in charge of the class were loud and overbearing and insulting, and they were like a dime a dozen, constantly roaming around, getting on you for nothing. Most of us knew it was just a big act, but that didn't make it any easier to put up with. When you were so pooped it seemed you could hardly move, you still kept going. About that time one of them would come over and say, "What the hell's the matter with you, soldier; you ain't even trying. Give me 50!" That meant 50 push-ups, so you got down and did as many as you could. The first and most normal reaction to all this was "I don't have to take this kind of crap from anybody." And we didn't have to take it because we could quit any time. But if you did decide to quit, you had to go up to the front of the class and take off your boots and socks. Then you walked barefoot back to the barracks. We were told anyone who quit would be sent to one of the infantry outfits that was ready to be shipped overseas.

The only way to get through jump school was to

survive both physically and mentally. You had to get angry enough to think, "Go ahead, you chicken-shit-bastards, I can take anything you got, so lay it on!"

At the end of the second day, the officer came to dismiss the class, but first he had to rant and rave a little.

"By God, I'm unhappy today, and I am damned mad. I thought they finally gave me some men to work with, but the sergeants tell me we got another bunch of softies. If there are any more quitters here you better get the hell out right now because I'm telling you that from here on, by God, we're going to start making men out of you."

That was the daily routine during the first week — exercise, judo, run, run, run and hot! By the end of the week it was beginning to get a little easier. But I was still beat at the end of the day and the muscles were still stiff and sore.

On Friday, when the officer came out to dismiss the class, we knew it was going to be some more of the same old crap, and it was.

"Well, by God, I'm surprised to see so many of you still here. But don't think you got it made because there are still 3 more weeks to go. And now I want to tell you something else. My sergeants have been trying to teach you some judo all week and they say some of you ain't doing too good. Well, by God, I tell you what. This weekend I want you to go into town and practice that judo on the MPs." That was a real stupid-ass thing to say.

The second week wasn't any easier, but it was better because if was different. There was still the calisthenics, the judo and the double time Ho! Run, Run, Run! No matter where we went, we never walked. Jeez! How I hated that double time Ho! It wasn't too bad to run here and there, but we knew that some time during the day there would be a run that lasted until we lost a few guys. Every day there were some who dropped out because they just plain couldn't hack it. There were a few who couldn't hack it but kept running until they blacked out and dropped. They were back with us again the next day.

During the second week the afternoons were different. There was a little relief from eight hours a day calisthenics, but not much, because nothing we did was easy. First there were the mock-up plane doors. When making a jump it was important that you be in the right position after you were out of the door, when the prop blast blew your chute out of the pack. The mock door was only 6 feet from the ground, so there was no problem! All we had to do was go out the door, make a quarter turn to the left, double over, and hit the ground on our hands and knees with our head towards the tail of the plane. No problem, right? Wrong. No matter how hard we tried, we couldn't do it right. We went out the door; we ran around the "tail of the plane" and climbed the ladder. Then we went out the door, ran around the tail of the plane, climbed the ladder and went out the door.

After an hour or so of jump out the door, we went to the next stage, which was either the cable tumble or the platform tumble. I'm sure those aren't the correct names but that is what I'll call them because it is the way I remember them.

The cable tumble was a very simple device. There was a steel cable about 150 feet long. One end was anchored to the ground and the other end was secured to a platform, about twelve feet above the ground. There were a couple of straps you grabbed before you left the platform. They were attached to a pulley that went down the cable, and away you went to hit the ground at 15 m.p.h. And, of course, about half way down, there was one of the sergeants who yelled either right tumble or left tumble. You damn well better do some kind of a tumble or you were going to go ass-over-teakettle, and you would probably get a mouth full of hot sand.

And then there was what I will call the platform tumble, another very simple device. You climbed up a ladder to a platform about 3 feet by three feet that was fifteen feet from the ground. Here the object again was to learn how to tumble when you hit the ground. If you jumped off the platform and were coming straight down, when you hit the ground it was very difficult to execute a tumble — chances were good you would just whop your chin against one of your knees. So when you jumped from the platform, you went out as far as you could to get a little forward motion. When you left the platform face first, you did a right or left front tumble, and when you left the platform butt first you did a rear tumble. And that was the second week, along with the perpetual "Double time Ho! Run, run, run," of course.

The third week was more calisthenics, judo and running, and we went from the 15-foot platform to the 250-foot towers. And yes, it was still hotter than

Hades. When our fatigues were wet with sweat it felt good because any little breeze had a cooling effect. We ate salt tablets like they going out of style, and while we were washing them down with a drink of water, we held our wrists under the faucet. We were told not to do that because there was a possibility the sudden cooling down of the blood could kill. That didn't stop us, because we knew that if we were dead, we would at least be cool.

Besides that there would be another perhaps small but definite advantage — if you were dead, you wouldn't have to go back to that stinking mess hall again. The evening meal was the worst, and Jeez! I can remember it like it was yesterday. I was hot and I was tired and I was so hungry I could hardly wait to eat. Even after run, run, run off and on all day, when I got to the mess hall I wanted to run again before I puked. It was a smell unto its own. It didn't really smell like garbage, and it didn't really smell like food — it just had a stench all of its own. What it came down to was that whatever they gave you to eat, you ate it and got out before you did puke, because there weren't any seconds. Those army cooks were something else. They didn't have to kill the hog, but they sure could murder a pork chop.

We lost quite a few on those 250-foot towers. There were the "controlled" towers and the "free fall" towers. We went first to the controlled towers, where there were cables and wires going from the ground to the top of the tower. Everything was controlled and we knew nothing could go wrong, but it was still scary, and there were quite a few wipeouts. I still don't think that was anything to be ashamed of, because there are many who just can't take heights. There were a variety of feats we had to perform, but there was one I really hated. They strapped us into a chute harness, and then we lay face down on the ground while they fastened a snap to the back of the harness. Then it was up you go, in a horizontal position, face down. When we were at the top, we waited for the sergeant to yell, "Pull!" Then we pulled the ripcord that released the snap on the back of the harness. After falling about twenty feet there was a sudden stop, and then we were lowered to the ground. There was one little gimmick to show we weren't scared out of our wits. The ripcord was pulled with the right hand, and while we were falling it had to be transferred to the left hand.

From these towers we went to the "free fall" towers. Here we buckled into a harness suspended below a chute that was already open and fastened to a huge metal ring. So then it was up you go until the ring hit the top of the tower, where the chute was automatically released, and then it was down you go. There were no control wires; you were on your own in a free fall. The primary objective was to keep your feet together and hit the ground with both feet at the same time. Never look at the ground below you — always watch the horizon. That was the cardinal rule, because for some reason when you watched the ground "coming up" at you, the natural inclination was to reach out to the ground, and if you did that you almost always hit the ground with one foot first. When you did that, you always hit like a ton of bricks, and often ended up with a bad sprain or a broken bone.

If we had learned how to tumble, which we had

by this time, there was no problem with the free fall, with one exception. If there was a strong breeze blowing, it would catch the chute at the moment of release from the tower, and when this happened we would be oscillating like the pendulum of a clock. And whether we were swinging from the front to back or sideways, it didn't matter, we would hit the ground like a ton of crap.

They did have some kind of system for monitoring the wind speed. If it was *at the limit of safety* or below, we went for a free fall. If it was above the limit of safety, we went for a run, waiting for the wind to die down. The only problem was that in order to complete the 3rd week, we had to do a free fall. So what it boiled down to was that on Friday, wind or not, broken leg or not, we made a free fall.

There is one more thing I should tell you about the third week. Each afternoon we spent a couple of hours learning how to fold and pack a parachute. And on Friday, *we packed the chute we were to jump on Monday morning!* We were told many times that the one thing we didn't have to worry about was whether or not our chute would open. They were like Ivory Soap, about 99.9 percent foolproof, and besides, if ours didn't open, all we had to do was bring it back and get another one. This wasn't exactly what one would call mental stress, but the idea of packing your own chute for your first jump was definitely not a comforting thought.

So we finally start the fourth week in jump school. We had to make five jumps to qualify. The schedule was to make one jump each morning, then come in and pack our chutes for the next day. It might seem like this would be the time for separating the men from the boys, but it wasn't. Most of the guys who had guts and the will to make it this far went all the way.

On Monday morning we strapped on our chutes and waited to go. When our turn finally came, after what seemed like forever, about a dozen of us got on the plane and it headed for the drop zone. The jumps and repacking the chutes took most of the morning each day. The main reason was because we jumped one at a time. When we reached the drop zone the plane flew in a big circle and each time we were over the drop zone, another jumper went out the door. The next guy would stand up and hook up and stand in the door, waiting for the jump sergeant to yell, "Go!"

We jumped from about 1,200 feet and when I stood in the door I could look down and see the red crosses on top of three or four ambulances, or meat wagons, as we called them. That wasn't a comforting sight, but it was good to know that if anything did go wrong we wouldn't be lying out there to bloat in the hot sun.

We all sweat all day long under the hot sun, but every morning before our jump, there was a little extra what we called "sweating it out" period. It may not have hit all of us, but I am sure it happened for most of us. It was more like "butterflies in the belly" and it was strange how each guy had his own time. Some would have big trouble buckling the straps on their chute harness, but as soon as it was done they settled down. For others the butterflies came after they had their chutes strapped on and were sitting around waiting to get on the plane. After they were on the plane, all was fine. It hit others when the plane was in the air and they were waiting for their turn to jump. When they stood up and hooked up, all was fine. The butter-flies started flitting for some when they were in the door waiting to jump.

I can remember only two things where we were given any leeway. One was when the sergeant said, "Give me fifty!" If we could do only forty push-ups, that was O.K. The other was when we were in the door waiting to jump. When the plane came over the drop zone and the jump sergeant yelled, "Go!" we did our best to go. But this was what might be called the "point of no return." And sometimes that best wasn't quite good enough. When we didn't go out the door the first time around, the plane would circle and there was a second chance to go. I don't think this hap-pened often – at least it didn't happen on any of the times I jumped.

For me, there was no "sweating it out" until I was ready to hit the ground, and I know this was because the last time I went off the free fall tower I sprained my ankle. It was my own damn fault because I reached for the ground and hit with one foot first and when-ever you did this, something usually happened. Not always, but you needed both feet to support you.

The afternoons during the fourth week were more calisthenics, judo and run, run, run, but by now that wasn't so rough. I think this was partly because we were in much better physical condition and also be-cause, at this stage of the game, they wanted us to make it all the way. The runs were always hard, but now there was a difference. Instead of "Come on you gut-less bastards," it was, "Come on, hang in there man, you can make it."

There were two criteria to be met during the fourth week in jump school. One was to make your five jumps. It would seem as though that might be enough, but on the last day, after making the fifth jump, and during the hottest time of the day, there was a nine-mile run around the airport.

Every morning during the last week I went on sick call, and the medics would retape my sprained ankle. When I put my boot on, I laced it up as tight as I could and there was no give. It felt a little like I was walking on a wooden foot, and there wasn't much pain.

This reminds me of something I haven't thought about for a long time. When we reported for sick call, there was a big bunch of us because I wasn't the only one stupid enough not to do it right. There were many injuries from top to bottom, like from sprained ankles to wrenched knees to sore tailbones, bad backs and necks. When we were all "present and accounted for", we lined up and began our march to the medics. It wasn't really a march, but it must have been a sight to behold. There were always a few on crutches. They went hippety-hop as best they could, while the rest of us limped along and did the best we could. All of us were hurting one way or another, and I was one of the lucky ones, because I was able to go on sick call and then go out and make my jump. The memory that comes back to me now is that because of the way we hippety-hopped and limped down the street, sick call in jump school was also known as the "Paratroopers

Shuffle." This was a very appropriate nickname, intended to be humorous, but it sure as hell wasn't funny.

I think my story is beginning to lag a little and I don't want to bore you, so I will move along. I made my five jumps and I made the nine-mile run around the airport. They gave me my wings and they also gave me another pair of boots. It was hard work on a new pair of boots, but I put a spit and polish shine on them like you wouldn't believe.

4

My next assignment was camouflage school. Each morning they taught us some of the basic principles of camouflage, and in the afternoon we went into the field and applied our new knowledge. There were some old beat-up Jeeps and trucks scattered around out in the sand, and we were to camouflage them so they would be hard to spot from the air.

We were divided into groups, and each group had its own project. The last thing we did each day was to go up in a C-47 and observe our project from different altitudes. On Friday, we put the finishing touches on our projects, and then went to the plane. We were supposed to make several passes over the area, at altitudes from a thousand feet to ten thousand feet.

There were only about a dozen guys on each plane because we all had to get to the door to make our observations. Some of us would lie on the floor with our heads out the door and others stood so they could see over us. So we got on the plane and the pilot taxied out to the runway. When we got to the starting line the pilot turned the old girl in the right direction, pulled back on the throttle and poured the soup to her, and we went roaring down the runway. Then he really gave her the gun and we knew we would be taking off any second. But we didn't get off the ground, and we were still roaring down the runway when the pilot backed off on the throttle. He didn't chicken out — he just used his head.

We were approaching the end of the runway and there was no way in hell we could get off the ground in time. When we got on the plane, we taxied our way to the starting line, but now, when the pilot turned the plane around, we rattled our way back to the starting line. I know that pilot would have been a good paratrooper because he sure as hell had more guts than he had brains. We gave it another to and this time we went airborne. About then I was thinking about what had happened and I was sure wishing I had a chute. Even though I kept telling myself nothing was going to happen and this wasn't why they call the C-47s "flying coffins." I still wished for a chute.

We made several passes over the area and were probably up to four thousand feet when we started down. We were supposed to go up to ten thousand feet, but the pilot told us later no way was he going to try and get that thing up any higher. That was my last memory of camouflage school, and it was the last time I used any of what I had learned there except to stick a few reeds in the camouflage net on my helmet when I came down in the water in Normandy.

The main part of Fort Benning was in Georgia, but there was also what they called the Alabama Area. That was where they sent us while we were waiting to be assigned to an outfit.

To get there we had to cross the Chattahoochee River, which was the boundary between Georgia and Alabama. To do this we had to take what was called a ferry, which was in reality nothing more that a big scow that was powered by the river current. They angled it one way to go east and the other way to go west, and it moved so slowly we sometimes wondered which way we were going.

I have several memories of the Alabama Area and the first is that it had to be one of the most God-forsaken places I ever saw. Nothing unusual about that, of course, because whenever the Army was looking at a site for a camp or a fort, the first specification was it had to be the most miserable and lonely area available.

During the week it was easy to get a pass into town. That would have been a real good deal except for one small hitch — we had to leave camp through one of the gates in the main camp. This meant we had to take the ferry across the Chattahoochee, which was little like taking a "slow boat to China." When we reached the yonder shore, and were so fortunate as to find a camp bus loading for a trip into town, we were lucky, since there would probably be time for 2 beers before heading back to Alabama!! If there wasn't a bus available right now, or if we had to wait for the next trip on the ferry, *forget it!* There was no way in hell we could bet back to Alabama in time for bed check at midnight! If you had a weekend pass, time was no problem, but for some reason, weekend passes out of Alabama were as scarce as hen teeth. I didn't have any difficulty coping with that situation because I had gone out on pass once during jump school, and that was enough. It was disgusting if you were sober. There was Columbus and there was Phoenix City and I think both were similar to Klondike during the "gold rush." If you wanted to get drunk and get into a fight, you could go to Columbus. On the other hand, if all you wanted to do was get drunk and get into a fight, you could go to Phoenix City.

The Alabama Area was sand and sun and hot,

hot, hot and it was there I got to be known at the "KP kid."

The Army had two kinds of police. The most honorable, of course, was the Military Police (MPs). And then there was the Kitchen Police (KPs). The MPs used their clubs keeping order, and the KPs used their knives peeling potatoes. They also scrubbed the mess hall floor, cleaned the greasy pots and pans, washed the dishes, and set the tables. I shouldn't say this is what "they" did because this is what I did. I volunteered for KP, and I still think it was the smart thing to do. It could very well have been an error on my part, but while the other guys were out there doing calisthenics and "Double Time Ho!" in the sand and the sun, I was sitting in the shade peeling potatoes. And there was another plus — the cooks and I had some delicious steaks before they had to cut them up for stew. Believe me, I never went to bed hungry.

If I were writing a book, there would be many chapters missing, because I don't have that many memories. There have been so many books written about World War II, which is now ancient history, there would be nothing I could say that hasn't already been said.

The Alabama Area of Ft. Benning was what I think the army called a "staging area." All of us there were merely making time, waiting for the cue as to when or where we appear in the next act. We were ready to go, and all that remained was for us to be assigned to an outfit. I was ordered to report to the 508th P.I.R. in Camp Mackall, NC.

I don't remember how long I was in Alabama,

but it was long enough for me to make my first night jump. It was made with a full field pack and all equipment except for ammo. I went out the door, my chute popped open and all was fine. I had it made. But then I realized I was swinging back and forth under my chute like a pendulum on a clock. That wasn't good, and I did the only thing I could to stop swinging. When I reached up as far as I could and pulled down on the lines, it would spill some air from my chute, and I would start dropping straight down a little faster. Whether I pulled down too many lines or whether I pulled them down too long, I don't know, but I was dropping fast when I hit the ground.

When I came to I was lying on my back, and I realized right now where I was. The first thing I had to do was get up and get out of the chute harness, but while my brain was alert, nothing else would move. The next few minutes were not good ones. I was counting the stars; I was wishing I was back on the farm, and of course, I was wondering what in hell was wrong with me that I couldn't move.

But all is well that ends well. I got on my feet finally, picked up my chute, and headed for the assembly area where the trucks were waiting to haul us back "home." I am sure I hit the ground on a backward swing, because the only bruises I had were on my butt, and my neck was a little stiff and sore. The sore neck probably was caused by my head hitting the ground so hard I blacked out for a while.

Within a few days all my hurts were gone and physically, I was back to par excellence. There could have been some permanent brain damage when my head hit the ground, and whether or not I had a complete mental recovery could be debatable.

5

I t was probably some time in August 1943 when I was assigned to the 508th P.I.R. in Camp Mackall. For me it was a good feeling to be in Company H, 3rd Battalion. It was almost like having a home away from home. Not quite, but after about nine months in the Army, I finally had my own outfit. And what a company we had — those guys were the best!

The training in Camp Mackall was intense. It had to be and we knew why, even though we didn't always like it. It went from intense to *rough* when we left camp for maneuvers in Tennessee.

Military maneuvers are designed to simulate actual combat conditions. During the Civil War, the blue and the gray armies roamed the Tennessee hills. My great grandpa Darton may have climbed some of the same hills I did. We were divided into the blue and red armies.

We were only simulating war games and combat conditions, of course, and I don't believe there were any of us who had every experienced actual combat. But there were at least a few who had a good idea what it would be like, and they tried to let us all know by making the maneuvers as rough as possible.

Our mess hall kitchen was now on wheels, preparing meals in the field, and bringing them to us. The drivers and the cooks were thoroughly briefed on the location of our bivouac area — they knew exactly where it was on the map, but there was still a problem. We were always out in the boondocks, and not only were all the country roads that would their way through the hills crooked as a ram's horn, many of them were nothing more than trails. So there was still a problem, because even though they knew exactly where we were, they still had to find us. Actually, *the one thing they knew* was that we were somewhere to hell and gone back in those damn Tennessee hills! Despite the adverse circumstances, they did bring us quite a few hot meals. Usually it was supper, and it might be served anytime between 6 P.M. and midnight.

It was always late in the afternoon when we arrived at the bivouac area, so the first thing we did was pitch our pup tents. And even though we were simulating combat conditions, those tents had to be lined up as straight as a carpenter's chalk line. If the chow line was set up before our tents were set up, we grabbed our mess kits and got in line because we were *gut hungry*. If there was no chow line by the time we had our tents pitched, we hit the sack because we were *dead tired*. When you are sleeping, you don't think about how hungry you are.

I remember so well the breakfasts. The pancakes, the eggs and the bacon were delicious! Delicious, but there was never quite enough in our mess kits fill our bellies. The coffee was hot, but for some reason, it always seemed to be a combination of battery acid and panther piss. You could drink it if you had a cast iron stomach, but most of us used it to rinse our mess kits because it did a good job of cutting the grease.

I also remember how the officers ate their breakfasts. There were board planks, about twelve inches wide and twelve feet long, raised about a foot off the ground on blocks. Each place setting consisted of a napkin, an upside down dinner plate from the mess hall on top of which there was an upside down cup from the mess hall on top of which there was an orange. Those poor guys not only had to sit on the ground while they were served, they also had to peel their own oranges. It is now forty-seven years later, but I can see that board plank "banquet" like it was yesterday. Perhaps I am not quite the compassionate person I like to believe because as I reminiscing I still have some of the same feelings of disgust I had then. I don't feel too uncomfortable about that for the simple reason that, what the hell, after all, we were supposed to be simulating combat conditions.

After breakfast we broke camp and packed our gear, and then went through the line to fill our canteen and pick up our brown paper bag. While it might be possible the army originated the brown bag lunch, ours were nothing like those carried by so many today, for at least two reasons. First, it never varied, so we didn't have to look and see what was in the bag – we knew it was an apple and a peanut butter and jelly sandwich. Second, that wasn't our lunch; that was our rations for the next twenty-four hours.

During those next twenty-four hours, we could chow down any time. The choice was ours, but there better be a wise choice. We left camp with full bellies and full field packs, and then we hit the road, sometimes marching along and sometimes at "Double Time, Ho." When the enemy suddenly started dropping artillery shells on us we had to hit the ditch and crawl on our bellies for long enough to get out of range of the artillery. I have no idea how they decided who died and who survived, but I was one of the lucky ones who had to live on.

The pancakes we had for breakfast stuck to our ribs almost as good as oatmeal, but by noon they were well digested and we were hungry. I would be thinking about my sandwich, but I was also remembering there was still another eighteen hours before the next meal — perhaps longer if the mess truck had trouble finding us again. During one of our breaks, the guy next to me decided to eat his sandwich, but first he peeled off all the crust and threw it on the ground. I made a quick move and before anyone else could get it, I picked it up and ate it!

The apple I ate one bite at a time. One bite because I was hungry and one bite because the juice quenched my thirst. The canteen of water had to last for twenty-four hours, so it had to be consumed sparingly. Even though we were simulating combat conditions, we still had to shave every day. I tried the "dry" shave a few times, but even with my tender whiskers, it felt like I was pulling them out by the roots.

We passed by many farms, but their wells were strictly "off limits." We also saw some little old country stores, and they were also "off limits." The idea of sneaking in and coming out with a few candy bars and a coke was very tempting, but it was also very ill advised. However, it was also a challenge, and some of us were lucky and some of us got nailed.

We spent a month on maneuvers — a month of being hungry and thirsty and a month of sweating and stinking, and I do mean stinking! We had one shower.

When we went back to Camp Mackall it was time

to pack up for a furlough home and for a trip "over there." Time-wise it wasn't a good deal, because they gave me two weeks and I gave them two years.

6

Our Port of Embarkation (P.O.E.) was New York City. We boarded ship during the night. Even though it was secured to the dock, our ship had a slight rolling motion — however slight, it was enough that when we cast off and set sail for sea the next morning, some of our guys were already heaving their seasick guts.

The Kraut submarines were having a hey-day, sinking many ships in the convoys crossing the Atlantic. Ours was a huge convoy, including the battleship Texas, three aircraft carriers and several destroyers. There were ships in every direction as far as we could see. Our ship was the USAT "James Parker." We left New York on December 28, 1943, and went into the harbor at Belfast, Northern Ireland, on January 9, 1944.

There were several guns mounted on the deck of our ship, manned by navy personnel. On the first day out we were told that the Navy wanted volunteers to keep a twenty-four-hour watch for Kraut subs or planes, and to carry up ammo for the guns if we had a problem.

One of the first things that a G.I. learns is *never* to volunteer for anything. I have no idea why, but I volunteered and it was one of the smartest moves I could have made. I was excused from all of the routine regimen and, even better, my special armband gave me access to the kitchen twenty-four hours a day.

We were as crowded on that ship as sardines in a can. So much so that there was time for only 2 meals a day. The line for breakfast formed at daybreak. It went up and down and round and round. They stood in line, and they sat in line, and they played craps in line, waiting for their green scrambled eggs. The eggs weren't really a deep green; they were just kind of light yellowish green. Breakfast was served by about 10 A.M. or 10:30 A.M., and there wasn't much to do to pass the time expect shoot the bull or throw the dice. Space on the deck was rationed because there were so many of us, but that was no problem. The north Atlantic is a bitter cold place to be in December. It was fun to watch the seagulls for a few minutes but that was about it. The gulls were with us all the way from New York to Belfast.

We stood watch four hours and then were off for eight hours. Day or night, it was always a long cold 4 hours, but it was time well spent. The mess hall for the ship's crew was open twenty-four hours a day, and there was always hot coffee and something to eat. I spent a lot of time there.

On New Year's Eve we all got in line and they gave each of us a shot. We couldn't name our poison because it was the same for everyone — a typhus shot.

My place for standing watch was the rear of the ship where I could see the wake as it rolled and splashed. In the black of the night, it had an almost fluorescent glow, and it was as fascinating to watch as the flickering flames of a campfire.

Seasickness was like a plague for the guys who had it and it was a stinking mess for the others. I was lucky, but there were a few times when I had to swallow hard and fast. When I had to go, and was headed for the "Head" I crossed my fingers. If the "Head" was cleaned, fine! But if there was some vomit swishing back and forth across the floor with each roll of the ship, there were two choices — if you could wait, you waited, and if you couldn't wait, you took your chances of staying on your feet while you were sliding across a floor that was as slippery as wet ice or a greased doorknob.

British navy tugboats guided our ship into the harbor when we arrived in Belfast, Ireland. I was on the deck when some of the British sailors boarded our ship, and even though I was close enough to hear them clearly, I sure had trouble understanding plain English.

From Belfast we went via a narrow gauge railroad to Port Stewart, a small Irish village that was like a miniature Coney Island. During the summer months it was a popular place for spending the "holidays." When the fall season arrived, 90 percent of the population went back to wherever they had come from and the other 10 percent remained behind to roll up the sidewalks and then go into hibernation for the winter.

There were two cafes open for business. Why they were open I have always wondered, because no matter whatever I ordered from the menu was always sold out! The only thing available was "chips" (French fries as we know them).

There was a theater where they showed movies two nights a week. This was the main center of attraction, for here we could go and see the movies we remembered from our childhood. I didn't see my old favorites, Ken Maynard and Hoot Gibson, but I did see Tom Mix. I have always been thankful I went to

see the movie "China Seas" starring Clark Gable and
Jean Harlow. Not because the film was so great, but
because of what happened when I came out of the
theater.

When the movie ended, we exited the theatre via
a long narrow hallway. It was very dimly lit, but when
I went outside my eyes still had to adjust to the complete darkness before I could see anything. I have never
seen nights that were darker that those winter nights
in Ireland. I had moved aside to make room for those
behind me, and while I was standing there I felt a touch
on my arm and a female voice asked, "Please, Yank,
will you come to my home?" I guess I was too surprised to answer her, and she said, "Please, Yank, my
husband I are here with our children. We all want to
meet one of you and we hope you will come home with
us."

I did go with them, and I am sure the kids stayed
up long past their bedtime that night. Terrence was 7
years old and Bridgett was 9. Their dad had been a
banker in Belfast but had transferred to the bank in
Port Stewart for the safety of his family. From that
night on, life in Ireland became much more bearable.
Their home was my home, and I enjoyed many evenings and weekends with them. I knew they were on
short food rations, but I did have quite a few meals
with them. Partly because they insisted I be there,
and also because it was hard to turn down a home
cooked dinner. I always had a feeling of guilt because
I knew they were sharing their food with me, but I
never went empty handed. A little sugar, tea or coffee
along with some candy bars for the kids helped ease

my conscience.

We lived in metal Quonset (Nissen) huts and our camp was a short distance from Port Stewart. I remember, Oh! How well I remember how warm and comfy-cozy we *weren't*. In each hut there were two stoves, about eight inches in diameter and three feet high. They were good stoves and would have performed admirably had they been given half a chance.

There was one similarity between those stoves and the G.I.s — both had to have good fuel in their bellies to perform. Our fuel wasn't delicious, but it was nutritious. We had plenty of fuel for the stoves too. It was called coal but this was definitely a misnomer because it was at least 80 percent slate — four shovels of coal in and three shovels of klinkers out. When the draft was open, the fire burned but the heat went out the chimney, and when the draft was closed a little the fire went out. The Irish farmers came into camp with gunnysacks full of peat, cut into blocks about the size of bricks. The peat didn't help very much. They didn't come to camp every day and when they did come there was never enough to go around. If our hut was lucky and got a full bag we split it and had a good hot fire in both stoves. There was no way to conserve it because it was bone dry and it burned like paper. We just kept stuffing in and those little stoves rumbled and roared and literally jumped up and down for perhaps an hour. Then the peat and the heat were gone and the hut cooled down again. I do believe we were provided the best facilities available and I think we knew this even though we were bitching. For some reason a G.I. seemed to be a little happier and content when he was bitching.

The winter climate did put a limit on our training exercises, but we were kept busy, and when we came back to camp after a day in the field, those huts were *cold!* Too cold for comfort, but never too cold for some poker or craps. When you started a game or found one where you wanted to sit in, you first wrapped a blanket around you and then got into your sleeping bag (fart sack). No problem. I didn't gamble, but for me there was no problem either. I spent many of those evenings sitting by the fireplace in my new "home."

7

It was early in March 1944, when the 508th departed from Port Stewart, and even though our destination was a deep, dark secret, we could only be headed for England. We were happy to leave behind us the metal Nissen huts and the miserably cold and damp North Ireland winter, but we would have been jumping for joy if we had known what lie ahead for us.

The move from the barrens of North Ireland to merry old England was like going from darkness to daylight. Our new home was a tent city in Wollaton Park and we couldn't believe it! It was too good to be true, and there was no way it could last! In addition to being a beautiful spot, the park was in the city of Nottingham, only about two miles from the center of what was the fourth largest city in England. It had to be one of the biggest mistakes the top brass ever made! That was what we thought at first, but then we knew they were only trying to provide the best for the best.

Wollaton Park included about seven hundred acres and was completely enclosed by an eight-foot high brick wall. The old Lord or Baron or whoever it was that chose that location to establish his estate sure knew what he was doing because it was beautiful.

Our regimental tent city covered only a small portion of the park. The main entrance to camp was a huge iron gate built into the brick wall. The rear of the camp was enclosed by a wire fence, very well constructed, very formidable because of the sharp barbs, and virtually impenetrable to anybody except a paratrooper who had stayed out a little to long and found the gate closed. One of the things that helped many G.I.s to survive was their ability to "improvise." If there was something we needed, we made one or we stole one or we came up with a good substitute. When the gate was closed and we couldn't walk back into camp, we crawled in. There were a few well-disguised openings in the fence and we all knew where they were.

There was a small lake behind camp and beyond that a high hill and that was where the old boy built his home. The castle, constructed in the 13th century, was still there, but now, of course, it was a museum and not a home.

In camp, for each company, there were two rows of tents, with the company street between. The first tent on one side was the orderly room and the first tent on the other side was the supply room. On the other end of the company street, separated by a comfortable distance, of course, was the company latrine. Latrine was the army nomenclature for an outdoor john. Ours was probably a twelve or fourteen holer.

When we were in the park, there were still a lot of wooded areas and quite a few deer. The first wall to enclose the estate was built about three hundred years ago to keep out the local peasants and other poachers. It probably served its purpose well, but I doubt that it stopped Robin Hood and his Merry Men.

The brick wall and the barbed wire barricade served two purposes — the G.I.s were confined to the regimental area and also were protected from a Limey invasion. The citizens of Nottingham honored us in many ways. It could almost have been called the Wollaton Park Zoo because of the way they were lined up outside the fence from daylight to dark. They weren't there to toss peanuts to the monkeys, of course — some of them were probably there out of curiosity, but I am sure most of them were there because they knew why we were there and they wanted to welcome us and meet us.

It took us a few days to get settled down and organized in our new camp, and then the training exercises got intense. We knew why we were there, and although we had no idea when it was going to happen, we knew that some of us would die. That was reality, and it was probably one of the first thoughts for many of us when we came to in the morning. If it had stayed with us all through each day, life would have been, to say the least, somewhat depressing. There was really only one way to avoid this, so we worked hard and played hard and lived for today. This was probably the most natural human reaction under those circumstances, and I am certain it wasn't unique to our outfit. There were some reasons for the saying, "The Yanks are over-paid, over-sexed and over here." It was to be expected we would live it up a little — we deserved it after the three months in Ireland. But I still don't feel there was any justification for pulling out all the stops as so many did. There was never a day when I wasn't proud to be a Yank and a paratrooper, but there were a few times when I was ashamed.

There weren't any taverns in England, only pubs. Some of them were quite a bit like our taverns; some of them were more like our old saloons. There was the Hand and Heart, the Admiral Rodney, the Cricketers Arms, the Jolly Higgler, the Red Rooster; and a few dozen others. The Yanks literally took over the pubs and there was no consideration of the shortage of "spirits." Whether it was beer or ale or wine or brandy made no difference — everything was rationed. The pubs were open for a couple of hours at noon and I suspect that was when many of the locals enjoyed the peace and quiet of their favorite pub. The evening hours were 6 to 10 P.M. and bedlam reigned supreme. Not always, of course, but too often.

The mess hall started serving the evening meal at 5:30 P.M., but the gates opened at 5 for those who had passes out of camp and there was a mass exodus. It doesn't seem reasonable that after working your butt off all day, you would head for town without eating supper, but there was a very simple reason. If you were going to a café you had to get there before they ran out of whatever food was being served. If you were going to see a movie or a play, there was always a long line, or queue as they called them over there, and if you were to get a seat, you had to be there before they quit selling tickets. And, of course, if you were going to one of the pubs to soak up some suds, you had to be there before the daily ration was gone.

We didn't go to town every night because the training exercises were very intense and there were many over-night bivouacs. Also, when we were in camp, passes were limited to 50 percent. So, if we hadn't been out on pass for two or three nights, going without supper was the least of our worries.

I can remember so well the supper we all should have missed. The mess hall served some tainted food, and while I have to chuckle now as I think about it, it sure wasn't funny when "H" Company "exploded" during the wee hours of the morning. Despite a lot of cussing and their most valiant efforts, many of the guys just couldn't reach the latrine soon enough. It was what you might call a double-dribble affair — some had grabbed their steel helmets and were either kneeling over them or squatting over them. The company street was composed of cinders, and those cinders had so many sharp points no one walked on them without boots. You can be sure it wasn't fun to be out there trying to set a new record for the 100-yard dash with bare feet. Needless to say, all of those cinders were removed and replaced.

The evening hours for the pubs were from 6 to 10 P.M. but quite often they would close early because the daily ration of spirits had served. The booze and wine always petered out first, and from then on it was only beer. There was the "bitter" which was too bitter and the "mild" which was too mild. A mug that was half of each was about right, but when it was time for a refill you didn't ask for a "half & half" – it was "Arf and Arf, please." And when you heard a loud voice saying, "Time! Time, please gentlemen," that was it. Even though it might be only 9 o'clock, there would be no more sales and if you wanted another drink you had to move on and try to find another pub that still had a supply.

I have no idea how many U.S. Army units were stationed in the Nottingham area, but there must have been quite a few because wherever you went, the city was filled with Yanks. Apparently there was very little discrimination against Negroes. It didn't matter whether you were black or white, you were a Yank and all were welcomed in the same manner. This was a sore spot with many and there were frequent incidents of racial fights and brawls with sometimes a fatal shooting or stabbing.

One of those incidents started on a Saturday night. If we left camp via the rear gate there was a long walk through a wooded area before coming to one of the city streets. The path went through a beautiful part of the park, but at night it was so dark, it could have been called the "Black Forest." On this Saturday night, three of our guys coming back to our camp were jumped and clubbed. The next morning we were told that two of them were in the hospital and one was dead. Everyone knew there was going to be revenge and trouble, but on that Sunday morning, the gates opened at 9 A.M. as usual.

It was a beautiful day, and it was a while before any of the guards wondered why so many of the guys were carrying their raincoats. However it happened, I don't recall, but when a weapon was found under a raincoat, the gates were closed and all passes were cancelled, but it was too late.

There was an amusement park that was frequented almost exclusively by black Yanks. Most of the weapons and ammo that left our camp under the raincoats were used at that amusement park. There wasn't what could be called a massacre, but our regimental area was sealed until further notice. It was like a national disaster, but after about five days, all was back to normal.

In some ways Nottingham was like a home away

from home. Many new friends were made all over England, and in many instances it developed into more than friendship. The term "war bride" became well known.

There were probably many who thought fun and games were the primary aims of the Yanks, but this was definitely not true. There were games, of course, but the ones we practiced were war games. We did work hard on the games and we did try hard to have fun. But it was much more than fun and games, perhaps more like trying to live a lifetime in a few short weeks or months.

During the months we were in England, I could have searched out the records of some of my ancestors, the Drakes and the Dartons, but at that time I was much more interested in the future than in the past.

Then one day there were orders from headquarters, and we knew the day we had been waiting for had arrived. We put clean socks and shorts in our packs, along with probably a picture and some paper and a pencil to write home, and the rest of our belongings went into our duffel bags which were to be stored in the mess hall until we returned. We all had round trip tickets, of course, but there was always the possibility the return trip might be cancelled out. If this happened, you wouldn't be picking up your duffel bag, but you wouldn't be needing it anyway.

We were "sealed in" at the airport where we were quartered in huge hangers. The acoustics were positively terrible and ever little noise reverberated back and forth, almost with a vengeance, it seemed. When we were sleeping, the noise from the poker game usu-

ally didn't bother, but a crap game could be very dis-
turbing. However, this wasn't all bad. If you acciden-
tally let a cuss word slip out, it would echo back to you
at least twice. Believe me when I say we were constantly reminded to keep our language clean!

Those few days at the airport were busy, busy. We
were thoroughly briefed on the invasion of Normandy,
with information on the overall operation, but with
details for our individual unit operation. Ever day we
spent hours studying maps and aerial photos of our
DZ (drop zone) and the surrounding areas, trying to
memorize the significant landmarks. There were riv-
ers, roads, bridges, wooded areas, railroads, villages, and
churches with tall steeples. Some of these were our
primary objectives and others were simply for orientation once we were on the ground.

When the combat load of ammo was delivered
to each company, we rolled it into the large bundles
that would be attached to the belly of the planes. They
contained the machine guns and mortars, which were
to heavy to carry on a jump, along with the cases of
ammo. They would be released at the same time that
we jumped, and the chutes on the bundles were color
coded so the machine gun squads and mortar squads
knew which contained their weapons.

The last afternoon and evening at the airport was
something else. We had been issued some French
money, and one of the things we did was to get as many
autographs as we could on a piece of money. I used a
"Cent Franc" note and it was completely covered with
names. When I jumped in Normandy, I landed in an
area that had been flooded and the water washed out

many of the names. I still have the note but today there are only about a dozen names that are still legible.

We all had short hair cuts, but when we saw a buddy and decided his hair was still too long, we just whacked off some more of it. There wasn't much resistance because we used our trench knives, and most of us had them honed to a razor edge. By the time we were done the only guys that looked even half way decent were the ones that had shaved their heads, and there were quite a few of them.

All of our buddies were going in with us, but each of us had another very close and dear friend — our weapon. And now that the day of reckoning was at hand those dear friends were cleaned and oiled and wiped and cleaned and oiled and wiped with loving care.

For each weapon there was a prescribed number of rounds of ammo to carry into combat. This didn't sound like anywhere near what we would need, and since there was plenty available, we all picked up a little more. In addition to the ammo and the grenades, we all jumped with a land mine in our packs. We were loaded for bear. The land mine just about filled our pack, so it was a good thing our jumpsuits were covered with pockets. They were bulging with K-rations, grenades, and other miscellaneous items.

I think we were quite well adjusted mentally. Psyched up, perhaps, because this was what we had been working and training and waiting for. But there was a physical problem difficult to cope with. Before leaving Nottingham our jumpsuits were sent to be impregnated for protection from gas. When they came back they were stiff as a board and had a very obnoxious odor. They were airtight of course, so if you did nothing but sit on your cot you would sweat like a butcher. The more you sweat, the more you smelled, and the same for the suit. After the six or seven days we were at the airport this might have been a secret ally for the Kraut pigs. If they faced up wind and took a deep breath, they would have known where to look for us. Fortunately, bullets travel faster than the wind, and there was a hell of a bunch of those Kraut pigs that all of a sudden quit breathing.

8

It has been so long ago I can't remember exact times, and since it isn't important, I will use approximates. To take off and fly directly from our airport to the drop zone at Ste. Mere Eglise, the flying time would have been forty-five minutes. Our jump was scheduled for 2 A.M. but we took off at 10 P.M. because there were hundreds of planes leaving airports all over England and it would take quite a while to get into the proper formations.

Except for blacking our faces and checking our equipment, there was little activity in our hanger that last evening. We had been together for a long time, and I remember looking around at all those guys I knew so well. There was Latimer, Ecoff, Downes, Medford, Slagle, Vashon, Smith, Brown, DeSimone, Jakeway, Judefind, Kumler, Matthews, Delury, Hughes, Bundy and so many others. And although we each had our best friends and buddies, I know that night we were one as we had never been before.

There was a lot of talk and bull flying around, but what we were saying never touched on what we were thinking. We had been given orders that, until further notice, we were to take no prisoners. All Krauts and any others who resisted were to be killed. We talked about what a silly order it was, because that was exactly what we intended to do anyway. And then we talked about how we wanted to kill them. Shooting them between the eyes would be O.K. but a gut shot would be much more fun because then we knew the bastards would suffer for a while before they died.

Some of the guys were hoping for the chance to stick at least a few of them with their bayonet. I really didn't go for that idea, but the gut shot sounded good.

This was a first for all of us. We knew where we were going, and we knew that some of us would not be coming back. I knew I was seeing and talking to some of them for the last time. But who? Sometimes, as I think back, it seems a little strange that I was so much more concerned about the others than myself. I am sure it was the same with the others — nothing is going to happen to me — I'll be back!!

So you are talking big and strong and spreading the bull with a wheelbarrow, but what are you thinking about? I'll tell you. Even though it is June and you are there in the hanger in your hot sweaty jumpsuit, you are thinking about Thanksgiving Day and Christmas. You are thinking about your folks and your hometown and the high school baseball team. All these things you think about, but only when you're not thinking about *her*. You have kept every letter from her, so most of them are in your duffel bag in camp for safe storage. There was mail call and there was "male call" and those letters had top priority. It might be a long time until the next letter catches up with you, so when you were packing your duffel bag back in camp, the last two or three letters went in your pack. And now, every day in the hanger at the airport, you read those letters again and again while you are looking at her picture.

When it was time to go, we all had the same problem. After we had strapped on our chutes, we had to waddle over to the plane because there was no way we could walk with all that equipment. To board the plane we had to climb up about five or six feet on a ladder and that was something else! First, we pushed the guy ahead so he could get up to the next step and then we grabbed onto him to pull ourselves up. It took a bit of time and teamwork, but we made it, and the plane took off.

Even though we knew it would be a while before we jumped, we were in the air for what seemed like hours. The roar of the two engines on our C-47 was familiar, but it sure as hell wasn't like a lullaby, and there were no naps. And then all of a sudden all hell broke loose or so it seemed. We were flying between the Jersey and Guernsey Islands on our approach to the French Coast, and the flak from the Kraut pigs was our first taste of the real war. There was a lot of it, but nothing in comparison to what they threw at us later.

We were to jump at five hundred feet, which gave us a slight margin of safety over what was the normal minimum height for a chute to open. The drop zone was only a few miles inland, so when we hit the coast we were flying low, and the Krauts were throwing everything at us including the kitchen sink.

Another of the orders from headquarters was that every trooper would jump. Any able-bodied trooper who refused to jump would be shot and killed by the last one out of the plane!

When we finally, at long last, got the signal to "stand up and hook up" our plane was like a bucking bronco. I hooked my static line to the steel cable that ran to the tail of the plane. There was no way I could stay on my feet unless I hung on to that cable and the side of the plane. I was toward the front and was next to last of our "stick" and I was wondering if I would get out. When we got the GO light, it seemed like nothing was happening and I was thinking, "God damn it, let's go, let's go, let's get the hell out of this plane before it goes down!" When I finally got to the door, which took forever, no one had to push me out.

And right now I knew I had jumped from the frying pan into the fire. It was about 2 A.M., but the hundreds of white phosphorous flares floating on small chutes turned the night into day. The sight would have been spectacular if it had been part of a July 4th fireworks display. There were the flares, the flash and boom of the ack-ack, and the red of the tracer bullets as they zipped past. But that night, from our front row grandstand seat, it looked more like a nightmare in Technicolor. It was a field day for the Kraut pigs — like shooting fish in a barrel.

We were supposed to jump just before we approached an area that had been flooded by the Krauts, but I knew even before my chute popped open we had over-shot the drop zone — the reflection of the light from the flares showed the water was behind us. I knew this wasn't good, but it didn't concern me as much as it probably should have because I knew there was no way in hell I could hit the ground alive. The sky seemed to be literally filled with tracers, and between each of them were about a dozen regular slugs. Those that were moving right along were no problem because they were going away from you, but those that seemed to be floating along in slow motion were bad news

because they were coming your way — I still believe if
there had been some magical way I could suddenly have
frozen them in space, I could have crawled to the
ground on them.

There was water in front of me but it looked like
ground below me, and I expected to hit like a ton of
bricks because of all the equipment I was carrying. I
braced for the shock and it was a shock when there
was only a big splash. I had been fooled when I looked
down because of the reeds growing in the water. They
were as thick as the hair on a dog, and had grown to
about eighteen inches above the water so there was no
reflection from the flares.

9

I never did like diving, feet first or otherwise, and this one didn't go well. I did a bit of coughing and sputtering before I was finally able to get my feet on the ground and stand up. By that time the flares were gone and the night once again became night.

The first thing I did was to get out of my chute harness and pull in my chute so I could stomp it into the water and out of sight. That was no problem, because I was standing chest deep in water. I was alone and scared as hell. Misery likes company and the one thing I wanted then was to find some of the other guys. My plane had overshot the drop zone, but I figured that was where most of them would be. So I decided to head back across the water and find them. The water kept getting deeper and when I reached the end of the reeds, it was up to my chin. The next step I took dropped me in over my head and I had to use the reeds to pull myself back. So there was no way I could get to join my buddies. It really didn't matter because I learned later our outfit was scattered all over hell's half acre.

The first equipment I threw away was my gas mask. It was strapped to my leg and it had to go because it was bulky and snagged the reeds when I tried to walk. When I looked towards land I could see trees against the skyline. I was sure if there was woods there it would be Krauts, and it just didn't seem like that was the way to go, so I decided to work my way around to the other side where I knew I should be. It must have been about 3 A.M. when I started and when daylight came I wasn't more than two hundred yards from where I started. Just wading through water would have been bad enough, but going through those reeds was something else, like walking through four feet of snow without snowshoes.

My rifle had gone under water with me when I came down and when I started working my way around the lake, I held it up, hoping it would dry out. Before long I used it as a cane and a stick to push the reeds out of my way. Most of my equipment had been discarded. The land mine followed the gas mask, and then went the extra bandoleers of ammo that were like a chain around my neck. The K-rations were sealed in wax-coated cartons, but the only things I could salvage were the metal cans of eggs and cheese.

I was sure that at least a few of the guys who jumped before me had drowned in the deeper water and the trooper who jumped after me must have got it when he came down closer to shore. I had heard a few shots from either a Schmeiser or a Kraut machine gun.

I was about three blocks from shore, and I could see a couple of Krauts standing on platforms built high in the trees. It definitely wasn't a good situation and I sure was wishing I was back on the farm hauling hay. There seemed to be only one way to go so I kept working my way around the water to join the others.

I had broken off a bunch of reeds and stuck them in the camouflage net on my helmet. When I was moving I had to bend down to keep below the top of the reeds and after going a while I had to ease my aching back. I spread my legs so I could straighten up and stay below the reeds. This went on and on. I knew if

I could see them, they could see me and I was thinking, "You bastards, why don't you nail me and get it over with?"

My trail of broken reeds was as clear as the bear paths leading to the dump outside of Phillips, Wisconsin. I had been watching the shore and I saw the Kraut pig when he started wading into the water. He went out until he came to my trail and then started following it my way. I knew he was going to come right to me because I was too pooped to stay ahead of him.

I stood for a while, watching him. Each time he raised his head to look around he was a little closer. I pulled back the bolt on my M1, and there was rust in the chamber. There were millions of tiny green seeds in the water, from the reeds and when I ejected the cartridge, I could see there were seeds in the clip. I dipped the rifle in the water and swished it around hoping to rinse away some of the seeds. When water ran out of the barrel I knew it wasn't plugged, so I released the bolt and the next cartridge went into the chamber. Would it still fire? I would soon know because I had decided it was going to be either him or me.

All this took some time, and now the Kraut was close enough that I could hear him splashing through the water. I was ready to shoot the next time he raised up. It wasn't going to be a gut shot — I didn't want that Kraut pig to suffer. I wanted him dead right now. Up he came, but when I tried to zero in on him, there was one of those damn little green seeds in the rear peep sight. When he went down and started wading again, I blew the seed away. When he raised up again, I aimed for his chest and pulled the trigger. KAPOW!! What a beautiful sound — just like the pop of my chute when it opened. Then there was a *little* noise I enjoyed — he was only a few feet from me and I could hear the bubbles when he went down.

I had wondered many times what it would be like and how I would feel when I would have to kill another human being. That time came and went without a thought and I never wondered about it again. To me they were Kraut pigs and still are, because even though they were human beings, they were more like human animals.

The one think I wanted then was to get the hell away from there. I was sure they would get rid of me after what had just happened. I began wading again but even though the adrenaline was flowing, it wasn't enough to keep me going steady. I was keeping a close watch on the shore, and then one time when I had to stop and rest my aching back, I saw two Krauts walking into the water. They went out until they came to the trail in the reeds and then started following me. They weren't at all cautious, just kept coming until they found the Kraut I had shot. They stood there talking for what seemed like hours before they headed my way again.

If my legs would have moved as fast as the thoughts going through my mind, I could have outdistanced them easily. They were coming to me in a straight line, one squarely behind the other and I wondered if maybe I could get two birds with one stone. My M1 was one good gun, but I wasn't sure.

I headed toward the open water and then circled back to wait for them. They were really stupid, just kept coming with their heads up. When they came to where I had turned toward the open water, they stood there talking, and again it seemed like forever before they started on my trail. They were going away from me and KAPOW! KAPOW! I shot them both in the back. This was perhaps a little sneaky, but it sure did cut down the odds in a hurry. What had looked like it would be nip and tuck had turned out to be a piece of cake.

Once again I started to work my way, still hoping to get around to the other side of the water and find some of the other guys. Fighting a war all by yourself is not only very discouraging, it is also very lonely.

The woods ended and there were open fields where I could see some cows and farm buildings. I kept going for a while, but finally I was so pooped I decided to take a nap. It still scares me when I remember — the water was four feet deep but I just didn't care.

Then I looked toward the shore and saw some of our guys — what a welcome sight! I yelled and wave at them and headed for dry land. When I lost the buoyancy of the deeper water, I didn't have the strength to keep walking. When I dropped to my hands and knees and started crawling, a couple of them came out and helped me the rest of the way.

There were about twenty troopers and one of them was General Gavin – "Slim Jim" Gavin, Commander of the 82nd. I soon learned that we were indeed on the wrong side of the water and a long way from our DZ. Gavin was considering wading to the other side and I told him I had already tried that but the water was too deep. While he was very concerned about where to go and what to do, my concern was to get my wet boots and socks off because my feet hurt like hell. The soaked leather had probably stretched a couple of sizes so the boots were no problem — they came off easily. The socks were stuck to the bottom of my feet and I had to peel them off inside out. I almost puked when I looked at the bottom of my feet. There was no skin, just raw bloody meat.

We were there for a while until "Slim Jim" decided maybe we could find some others at a railroad bridge that was one of our objectives to destroy. One of the guys gave me a pair of dry socks. I put them on, slipped into my wet boots and we were on our way. It was like walking on a bed of hot coals, but no way were they going to leave me behind and alone again!

We found the railroad tracks and followed them. When we came to where the tracks were in a ravine with banks about 30 feet high, a scout was sent up on either side. We were approaching a vehicular bridge across the ravine when the scouts reported tanks and troops coming our way from the left, so we climbed up the right side to have a look.

The Krauts were about a half-mile away, coming our way on the road leading to the bridge over the ravine. On our side there was an old railroad track with a bed of dirt about five feet high and beyond that there was flat land for a long way. There was just time enough for us to conduct a hasty strategic withdrawal which means we ran like hell and scattered out behind the dirt bank.

The Kraut column stopped when the lead tank got to the bridge, and for a while they milled around and had a bit of a chit-chat. Apparently, with all of the wide-open terrain around us, they didn't suspect there were Americans behind that little old dirt bank. When the first tank started across the bridge, it looked like the war was over for us. Our chances were about the same as those of a snowball spending a week's vacation in hell.

Our heaviest firepower against those tanks with their 88's and machine guns was a B.A.R. Our B.A.R. man flipped the lever on his rifle to full automatic and when the tank was about half way across the bridge, about fifty feet away, he cut loose. We all gave them a quick three or four-round volley and one of us got the tank driver because it stopped and did a little turn so the bridge was blocked. And then all hell broke loose.

Those 88s must have had impact shells because it was Bang-Pow, Bang-Pow!! Those that went over us exploded in the field behind us, and when they hit the bank, we were showered with dirt. During the first lull, we heaved a few gammon grenades at the tank. The ground shook and it sounded like the bridge had collapsed. Then they opened up again, Bang-Pow, Bang-Pow!!

If they had dispersed the infantry and sent soldiers across the ravine to flank us, we would have been dead ducks. We expected that would happen soon, because they had to know from our limited firepower there were only a few of us. Then we heard planes behind us. It was a group of C-47s towing gliders.

They flew directly over us and the Krauts fired at them. The planes were flying low and some of them must have been hit, but none went down. It must have been at least a mile to the far side of the flats but we could still see the gliders landing.

When the Krauts did an about face and started after the gliders, we started shooting and we had some real easy pickings before they were out of range. We did our best because we knew the only good Kraut was a dead Kraut.

We had to be careful about the tank on the bridge, but there was not one in it except the dead driver. One of the gammon grenades had done a job on a wheel or gear on the track of the tank, so it would be a job to clear that bridge for use.

We headed for the railroad bridge again, and several times a few more of our guys joined us. From the way we had been scattered, it was for sure our jump hadn't gone as planned for many of us. There was shooting all around us, so we knew no matter which direction we went, we would find more troopers.

When it was too dark to see very far, we holed up for the night. There was no trouble. We took turns on guard duty but got some much needed rest.

The next morning, my feet were on fire. There were red streaks up both legs and lumps in my groin. Today, it would probably be just another infection, but back then it was a blood poisoning. After spending the first 16 hours in Normandy in the water, something had to develop. Shortly after daybreak, four more troopers joined us. They had spent the night in a first aid station only a few minutes away, and General Gavin told me to get there as soon as I could. I never saw the general again.

The medics had chosen a good site for the aid station. It was like a small fort. There was a courtyard with the farm home in one corner and the barn in the opposite corner, and the entire area was enclosed by a wall about six feet high. The buildings and the wall were solid, built with fieldstone and mortar. It was a little like a fort, but it was also not like a fort because the defense garrison was like nothing — medics who had no weapons and wounded troopers.

On my way to the first aid station, I was hurting bad and feeling sorry for myself, but that feeling didn't last long. Some of the troopers had what we called a good clean wound, but others had been shot up bad. Their chances of making it would have been good if they could have been evacuated to a hospital, but there was no place to go. Our medics were well trained, but in a first aid station set up in a French farmyard, there was only so much they could do, like iodine, sulfa powder and bandages.

I was sitting in an old straight chair, tilted back against the wall to keep my feet off the ground. There was only one opening in the wall where you could get in and out of the courtyard, and I was stupid enough to sit directly across from the opening. I could see across an open field to a woods on the other side. Somewhere out there, either in or behind one of those trees was a Kraut, and when he shot, my arm jerked. The bullet went through the elbow of my jacket, hit the wall and dropped beside my chair. I got out of the line of fire in a hurry. From the way my arm had jerked,

I expected to lose some blood, but when I rolled up my sleeve, there was just a red streak where the bullet had grazed my arm. He missed by six inches and if that Kraut had been using an '03' he probably would have got me good.

The fighting in Normandy was rough all the way from the beaches to where we jumped. It was several days before we learned the beach heads had been established, and though the situation still wasn't under good control, it seemed to be turning our way a little.

10

It was about July 15 when we returned to our base camp in Nottingham. Unlike the regular infantry, we did not get any replacements while we were on the line, and when they pulled us out; there were only thirty-five troopers in my company. We went back to the same company street, and even though it was familiar, it was never the same again. Nevertheless, I remember how thankful I was to be back.

I also remember one of my most painful jobs ever. When we left camp for the jump into Normandy, we took with us only the bare essentials, leaving the rest to be stored in our duffel bags until we come back. It was my job as company supply sergeant to go through the bags of those we knew would never be back, to separate the G.I. property from the personal items that would be sent home. Joe Bundy and Lewis Latimer and I had made the rounds in Nottingham many times, and now I had to toss the boots and uniform they had worn so proudly — I had to toss them on the piles of so many others. It was rough because every bag I opened belonged to a buddy or a friend. However much it hurt, I think it was a help and made me realize those guys were really gone.

The replacements who joined us in Nottingham were a great bunch of guys. They had to be because, what the hell, they were paratroopers. Once again we were back to full strength, and once again we trained hard and played hard. I know those of us who survived Normandy welcomed the training with a vengeance and a hatred that had no limits and we did our best to instill those feelings into the new guys. We had a lot of scores to settle, and we intended to do just that. From the middle of July to September 17 wasn't a long time, but when we jumped in Holland, we went in with a team of dedicated killers.

General Eisenhower addressed us to thank us for the good job we had done in Normandy, and to tell us he would be calling for our help again. He also told us we were his best combat soldiers and his worst garrison soldiers. We took this as a compliment and continued to raise hell wherever.

We were given a few days of grace to set up housekeeping and check in at our favorite pubs. When the training began they really laid it on us. We welcomed it because we wanted to be ready. Of course, we cussed and bitched, but now it was directed at those lousy Krauts – "You bastards, you started this thing but we are going to finish it!" A G.I. has to bitch about something to be happy. We did double time with a full field pack; we hit the dirt with a full field pack; and we marched with a full field pack until our feet hurt and our backs ached. We had no problem maintaining the proper attitude — KILL! HATE! KILL!

It wasn't all work, of course, and there were a lot of good times. Were they as good as before? I think so. After all, this was the second time around for quite a few of us who knew only too well that although life was good, it could also be short.

It has been so long that I don't remember whether it was while we were in Nottingham or later, but one of our training jumps was a disaster. When the "GO!"

light came on, the pilot cut the speed and raised the tail a little to be sure we cleared it on the way out. For some reason one of the planes lost altitude, and when it began to hit the troopers who had jumped from the planes ahead, the pilot turned the plane straight down and crashed. One of the guys in my company was a good artist. He had gone along for the ride to sketch the jump. He was on the plane that crashed. One of the troopers who had jumped went down when his chute was snagged by the tail of the plane. He stood up and was almost out of his harness when he dropped dead.

When we "policed" the company area, we picked up cigarette butts and any other litter. It was a grisly job when we went to "police" the drop zone after that jump. I picked up the toe of a boot that had apparently been sliced through the arch by a prop – the foot was still in it. The guy on my left picked up half of a billfold. Those last split seconds must have been terrible.

My battalion jumped the next day and all went well. It was a good jump and a happy day for us.

And so it went. We worked and trained and played until September, when we stored our duffel bags and left for the airfield. In some ways the days we spent there were similar to those last days before the jump into Normandy — rolling the equipment bundles, checking our weapons, shooting the bull, etc.

In 1984 there was a Dutch book titled *In Water en Vuur*, published to commemorate the fortieth anniversary of the liberation of the Beek-Ubbergen area in Holland. It was compiled by Margot van Boldrik with the help of a Dutch journalist, Daaf P. Wijlhuizen. In 1985, after many requests from those who could read only the pictures, a supplement was published in the English language. *In Water and Fire* contains material and pictures received after the original book was published and includes the Nijmegen area. One of the contributors to the book was Henry McLean, also from "H" Company, who told of an explosion on the airfield before we took off.

There was an explosion and I remember it well. We were taking the bundles containing our machine guns, mortars, ammo, land mines and other explosives, from the company areas to the planes. Two guys could roll or drag the bundles to the back of the truck and then they would drop about 4 feet to the ground. There was nothing dangerous about that because the bundles would hit the ground much harder when they came down on chutes.

But somehow, someone had fouled up and one of the bundles exploded. There was a terrific blast that demolished the truck and set two planes on fire. I don't know how many were killed, but one of them was a good friend, Bob Scheer. He was on the truck and was probably standing directly above the bundle. The only means of identification was a battered dog tag.

11

It was a sad way to start the day, but soon we were in the air headed for Holland. There was an escort of fighter planes and it was reassuring to watch them buzzing around us. The Kraut air force was no longer a big threat, but it wasn't kaput, and without our escort even a couple of their fighters could have meant disaster for our slow C47s. I can remember looking out and thinking we were flying over too much water. After Normandy, one thing I didn't need was more water!

That Sunday, September 17, 1944, was a beautiful day. It was about noon when we got the signal, and out we went for an almost perfect jump. Our drop zone was a huge field of red clover and the only water was a canal running through the field. Our entire 3rd Battalion was assembled and moved out in forty-five minutes.

I don't know whether or not the fighter planes escorting us had any bombs or rockets, but those flyboys sure did a number on the anti-aircraft gun that was set up on our drop zone. They must have hit it just minutes before we jumped because when we came down one of the Krauts was still alive, gasping for breath. He was hit bad and dying — we just left him there to do it his way. It was a bloody mess, but it was a beautiful sight to behold.

Before moving out the mortar and machine gun squads had opened some of the bundles to get their weapons and ammo. There were about a dozen of us in the battalion supply section and it was our job to get as much of the remaining equipment as we could off the field and set up a supply depot.

It was only a few minutes later when the sky was full of C-47s again, each of them towing a glider. The towlines were released and the gliders came down all around us. How different it was from Normandy. This time there was plenty of room for all of them to land in one piece. Each of them unloaded a jeep pulling a 57-mm cannon, and almost before we realized it we were alone again. But not for long.

Now I can tell you another of my good memories. All the while we were working we kept a close watch, because we had jumped fifty miles behind the front line and we knew the Krauts could come in quick. When we saw a few horses coming across the field in our direction, each pulling a cart with two big wheels, we didn't know what to expect. Were those carts full of Krauts? The horses were trotting and the drivers were waving their caps. We had only one choice — sit tight, wait, and hope. When they pulled up and stopped, we soon learned those Dutch farmers had come to help us. They worked with us, loading and hauling bundles to the supply dump. With their help I am sure we collected at least twenty times as much as we could have done by ourselves. Those Dutch farmers stayed and helped us until the Krauts started coming out of the woods on the far side of the field. We left the field in a hurry with our last cartloads of bundles. There were still some bundles on the field, but we had to forget about them. My first impression of Holland was those Dutch farmers, and I will never forget them.

We had set up our supply dump on a small hill, spreading it out amongst some big boulders, and from there we could see the Krauts coming out of the woods on the far side of the field. One of my buddies and I opened a bundle to get out a mortar and some 60 mm shells. When it is used in the conventional manner, with a base plate and a bi-pod, the mortar is a very accurate and deadly weapon. We were in a hurry, so while I held the bottom end of the tube against a big rock, my buddy began dropping in the shells. Our method of aiming was strictly by guess and by gosh, but we did quite well. We were using white phosphorous shells, the favorite ammo of our battalion commander. We could see where the shells landed because with each burst there was a beautiful shower of white-hot phosphorous, like a big umbrella. Whatever that stuff hit it burned its way in and stuck there. The Krauts were rolling on the ground trying to put out the fire, but I don't think it helped much.

The company that had been held in reserve was also pounding the Krauts, and while we slowed them down, there was no way we could stop them — there were just too many. They got to the drop zone and burned quite a few of the gliders.

Later I learned that my buddy was awarded the Silver Star for his gallantry in action during the counter attack on the DZ in Holland.

During the first few days our resupply of ammo and rations came in by plane, and dropped with chutes on the DZ. That didn't last long, of course, because we had jumped only fifty miles behind the front line and it didn't take long to open supply lines from the rear to our positions. But those first few days were very interesting to say the least.

The Luftwaffe was no longer a significant factor in the war but was still in business and whenever we went to pick up the supply bundles the Krauts made us a part of that business. Every time we went out we knew we would be strafed by Kraut fighter planes. They always came in low and would be on us before we knew it. There was never more than two of them, but that was enough to scare the hell out of me. A couple of times I was able to run for the canal, jump in, and stay under water as much as I could. Usually there wasn't time to do anything but stand and watch the bullets tear up the turf. The planes would make two or three passes and leave. Our supply section was lucky, and none of us were ever hit.

It was much different for the guys in my company. Their first objective was the small village of Beek. There were a lot more Krauts there than had been expected. After four or five attacks, the village was secured, but it was at a hell of a price. During the first twenty-four hours "H" Company went from 120 men down to 50 men. Snipers got at least 25 either in the head or through the heart.

After the supply lines from the rear were open, we had our full complement of vehicles, drivers and cooks. I mention cooks because our battalion commander, Colonel Mendez, had issued a mandate or decree or perhaps more simply an *order* that when his men were on the front line, they would have at least one hot meal a day. This wasn't always possible, and even though our cooks weren't jumpers, they sure found out what life on the front line was all about. The company kitchen was a truck equipped with several field ranges (stoves). It wasn't possible to take the truck to the front line so we took the food in the Jeep and trailer I used for hauling ammo and other supplies.

The company supply room was a large truck driven by Scott Ellsworth. Ammo and rations went from battalion supply to company supply to the line and most didn't stay very long in one place. When I wasn't hauling from battalion, I was hauling to the line.

When we were in garrison the ration for cigarettes was one pack a day. When we were in combat there was no ration — we didn't get them by the pack or by the carton. We got them by the case!

I will always remember the Jeep driver, E. C. (Easy) Evitts. What a guy and what a driver! He loved that Jeep, and between runs he was forever checking and cleaning and tuning it. I really believe it loved him too, because no matter how we had to abuse it, it never let us down.

When the fighting was heavy and the guys on the line needed ammo, we went right now. But whenever we could, we varied the time of our supply runs to the company. There were times when some of the route we had to take was under direct observation by the Krauts, and then we would go at night when we could. Usually we would take the trailer so we could haul some extra supplies. During the day we took only what we could load onto the Jeep because we had to be able to move especially when the mortar shells started looking for us. Evitts would yell, "Hang on!" and believe me I hung on. We went on the road, in the ditches, and across the fields. We couldn't get up much speed when the Jeep was loaded to the hilt with ammo, and I can still hear Evitts talking to the Jeep, sometimes cussing, sometimes begging, but always asking for more, "Just a little more, baby!"

After we had accomplished our primary objectives and the situation became stable, we spent more time in defensive positions. When we moved, the first thing we did was to dig in, and Scott Ellsworth and I always shared a foxhole for two. Scottie and I dug fast and we dug deep, and we always found a way to cover our new home with two to four feet of dirt. The finishing touch was to line it with a big piece of nylon I had cut from my chute so there was no dirt sprinkling down on us. It was still a foxhole, but it seemed more like a deluxe underground one-room apartment.

I remember one day when our supply section was set up in a large apple orchard. A few of us were sitting by one of the ammo trucks, shooting the bull (like all G.I.s did occasionally) and wondering why the Krauts were throwing so much artillery into a small village about a half mile from our position. We could hear their guns when they fired, and we could see the shells burst. Suddenly the sound of their guns was much louder and we thought, "Oh! Oh! that could be incoming mail" and we were right. Tommy Thompson and I took off right now, heading for our foxholes, but we didn't make it. To hell with *Double Time, Ho!* Tommy and I were side by side, doing *triple time,* when one of those shells came down through the apple trees and hit the ground about ten feet in front of us. We were dead! At least we would have been, but the shell was a dud. Tommy and I did a very quick "about face" and headed for where we had just come from when we realized there were no more shells coming our way. The Krauts had thrown four shells right into our laps and all four of them were duds. Miracles don't happen often, but I know they do happen.

We were listening for more shells when I started laughing. I guess it was maybe a little like sometimes you are so happy you cry, and sometimes you laugh when you are scared. Right about then I sure as hell was scared, but I had to laugh when I looked at Tommy — his helmet was on backwards. When we did that very quick "about face," he turned around but his helmet didn't.

There was one supply run Evitts and I made I remember well. All was quiet but we could hear something besides the Jeep. It was different and I am not sure where we heard it or felt it or both. When we looked up, we stopped and just sat there watching. What a sight, what a beautiful sight! The sky above us was full of planes. For a while, as far as we could see, from horizon to horizon, the sky was full of planes. The air and the ground seemed to vibrate. The shredded foil they released to confuse the radar on the Kraut anti-aircraft guns fell all around us. It did the job because we saw hundreds of ack-ack bursts without a plane shot down. Later we learned this was the first 3,000 plane raid on the German Kraut pigs.

It was while we were in Holland we first learned of the jet plane. The British had relieved us and taken over our defensive position while we went to Nijmegen for a rest period. Once again, the Dutch people welcomed us, even though we were dirty, and when I say dirty, I should say filthy — also cruddy. There had been a lot of rain, and the bottoms of our foxholes were mud and water. We had been issued some wooden pallets to put in the bottom of the foxholes, and even though they helped, there was no way we could avoid being mud from head to foot.

Getting off the line for a three- or four-day rest period was great, but when we were given access to a large school for hot showers and swimming in a big indoor pool, that was also great.

The sound of a jet plane is very familiar today, but when we heard it in Nijmegen for the first time, we were all wondering what it was. I doubt that any of us saw the plane because we were looking to the noise, which was, of course, far behind the plane. We did recognize the whistle of the bomb the pilot released, but the explosion was far from us. It was probably another attempt to destroy the Nijmegen Bridge, because it was the only vehicular bridge for miles up and down the Waal River. It was one of the objectives in the area and was captured intact. Demolition charges were in place and wired but apparently the Krauts wanted the bridge as much as we did and they waited just a little too long to destroy it.

We had accomplished our objectives, and the last days of our campaign in Holland were quiet. Quiet but still miserable, because there was rain and mud. We didn't get out of Holland until November 11, and by then it was getting cold. Being wet was bad enough, but being wet and cold was miserable.

While we were busy touring Holland, the rear

echelon was busy moving our base camp from Nottingham, England to Camp Sissonne, France.

12

When we left Holland we were fed to the gills — we were tired, we were dirty, we were cold and we were eagerly looking forward to sleeping on a cot instead of in a wet foxhole.

Our advance detail arrived in camp about 2:30 A.M. and after almost two months in the blackout at the front, it still seemed strange to be driving at night with the headlights on. There was a lot of activity because they knew when we would get there and they knew the rest of our guys would arrive in the morning. We had hot coffee and sandwiches waiting for us and they were welcome because when we got off the trucks at 2:30 A.M. on the morning of November 14, we were tired and cold and *hungry*. But the best news was that were would be a chicken dinner — a chicken dinner with *all the trimmings!!!*

The cooks were already busy working on the dinner because it was to be something special. There were probably about twenty stoves, and one each was a "G.I." can filled with chickens and boiling water. When I had my first cup of coffee and sandwich, I went over to stand by one of the stoves to get warmed up a bit and look at those chickens. They were smooth and plump, and I was thinking about how good it would be to dig into a leg with the skin fried nice and crispy brown. I was hoping there might be enough for seconds.

Suddenly, something didn't seem right, and when I looked at those chickens again, I couldn't believe it. The reason they were so plump was because they were being cooked guts and all. I have some good memories, some bad memories and some "chicken-shit" memories. The "G.I." can was what we now call a garbage can and those were sure as hell full of garbage.

After Nottingham, Camp Sissonne was like disaster. It was an old army camp, with all the buildings constructed of stone and mortar. It was old and it was cold and it was dirty rotten filthy. I guess the best way to describe it would be to say I think the Kraut Pigs used it during their occupation of France and it hadn't been cleaned since they left.

Training exercises started again, and it wasn't easy, especially for those of us who had just come out of Holland. We were much more in the mood for furloughs to Nottingham and passes to Paris than we were for night hikes around the French countryside.

It was a busy time for all, including the supply section. All of our weapons were sent to ordinance for repair or replacement. There had been a lot of equipment lost in combat, and we all needed winter clothes and blankets. I sent requisitions to the quartermaster by the dozen. I think the one thing we needed most was jump boots, the boots that were for paratroopers. We hadn't been issued any since we arrived overseas, and it was a real sore spot for every one of us.

Sissonne was a small village located next to an army camp so I guess it was only natural and to be expected there would be a "house of ill fame" and there was. The whorehouse was busy, but the bakery was a big competitor. Those long loaves of French bread were fantastic. It was almost more like cake than it was like bread, and if it was fresh out of the oven and still warm, it was delicious. There was never enough to go around so if you wanted to buy a couple loaves, you had to get there early. We would tuck them under our arm and break off a piece to eat while we walked around town. It was good. It was so good that when we met a buddy who didn't have a loaf we would break off a piece and give it to him. There was nothing to do except walk around, so I was back in camp before long. Always made sure to have at least part of a loaf of bread left for the guys who hadn't been on pass.

There were passes to the city of Reims, about thirty-five miles from camp. There was a plant in Reims where they brewed and bottled champagne, and we could buy it for thirty-five cents a bottle. The only hitch was we couldn't buy it at any price without an empty bottle to turn in. I don't know where all the empties came from to get us started, but the champagne sure did flow in Camp Sissonne.

We had been in camp for a month and were just getting comfortably settled when suddenly all hell broke loose. It was about 8 P.M. on December 17. I was at the movie in the motor pool building, and then there was a lot of noise outside. The movie stopped, the lights went on, and we were ordered to our company areas immediately. There we were told the Krauts had broken through the line with a huge attack in the Ardennes and we were leaving for Belgium in the morning.

13

We had no weapons, we had no winter clothing, particularly warm gloves, mittens or boots, and we had received none of the other equipment I had requisitioned. But *not to worry!* After all, we had learned a little judo back in Fort Benning, so if we couldn't shoot the Krauts, we might still be able to kick them in the ass.

The convoy of trucks that pulled into camp that night must have been at least a mile long, and now hear this: each of the trucks had two men in the cab and every one of them was wearing a pair of shiny jump boots! They had no idea what they were getting into when they jumped out of those trucks. We knew then why we hadn't been able to get anything but the combat boots with buckles on them, and for us this was a crock of crap. We gave them a choice — they could take off the boots or we would cut them off. So there was snow and it was cold and it was no time to walk around in your stocking feet. Our hearts bled for those guys, but very few, if any, of those boots left camp. After all, they wouldn't be hurting for long because as soon as they went back to where they came from, they would all put on another pair of our boots.

There was no sleep that night. We were busy opening cartons of weapons, ammo, clothing, and other equipment. There were weapons and ammo for everyone, but the supply of winter clothing was pathetic. There were some rubber goulashes and some packs with rubber bottoms and leather tops, but most of the guys had to go into winter combat wearing only leather boots. For our outfit, the Battle of the Bulge went from the middle of December to the middle of February. It was bitter cold, the snow was at times hip deep and there were more casualties from frostbite than from combat.

In the supply room, there were forms to record the G.I. equipment issued to each guy in the company, be it a pair of socks, a canteen cup or a rifle. But on that night of December 17, those records were forgotten. I just gave out the supplies as best I could. It was like first come, first served and if the coat doesn't fit, trade with someone.

There was no bed check that night. After working all night we were still trying to reduce the situation from pandemonium down to organized confusion when we left camp in the morning. We were loaded in huge tractor-trailer trucks, destination Werbomont, Belgium.

The trailers were built a little like the cars the railroad used for hauling coal. When we stood up we could just see over the side, but we didn't stand up very often. Partly because if we did the cold wind hit us in the face, partly because there wasn't anything worth seeing, but mostly because we were trying to get the cosmoline off our weapons. On a hot day in July or August, removing cosmoline is like breaking apart a chocolate cake with your fingers, very messy but fairly easy. When you are outside on a cold December day, removing cosmoline is one hell of a rough job.

Each trailer had a few cans of gasoline to be used in removing the cosmoline. If those cans had been filled with water it would have been frozen solid. But the gasoline just got colder and colder. First we soaked and then we scraped, then we soaked and scraped again. We could work only a few minutes at a time because our hands got so cold we couldn't open or close our fingers. We were tired as hell, we were cold as hell, and we were mad as hell. When we arrived at our destination and got off the trailers in the middle of the night, it was black as hell and we were ready to raise hell.

The weather had been unfavorable for some time — cold and snow, with cloudy sky and lots of fog. There hadn't been any activity on the line and it didn't seem likely there would be. This static situation may have had something to do with why a "green" outfit (no combat experience) was put on the front line. The 106th Division could at least get adjusted to living in the snow and the cold and send out a few patrols.

When Von Runsteadt launched his attack the 106th was one of the first American units to get hit. It wasn't wiped out, but the Krauts captured a lot of prisoners and vehicles. They used the uniforms and vehicles trying to infiltrate our lines.

When we heard that some of our guys had been cut down by "G.I.s", it became a very hairy-scary situation. When we saw some G.I.s through the woods or on the road, we didn't say, "Hi." We zeroed in and if we didn't get the countersign *right now*, it was POW! We for sure didn't want to kill one of ours, but we for damn sure didn't want to be wasted by one of those "G.I.s" either. The Krauts soon learned those tactics weren't working so that crap didn't last long.

But the *cold* and the *snow* and the *fog* seemed to

go on forever. When you are out in the winter twenty-four hours every day, when you leather boots are wet and your feet are freezing, when your gloves or mitts are wet and your fingers are freezing, *believe me,* it isn't just cold, it is bitter cold!

On December 21, we were on Thier-du-Mont, a ridge just south of Goronne, Belgium. That was where my buddy Bill Howe met Gabrielle. They were married later. I saw them about three years ago at the Busson Pig Roast in Ohio. Bill died a few months later.

When I think of the snow, I think of the vehicle we called a weasel. The body on ours was like a big box. There was a seat for the driver and the rest of the space was for supplies. It was equipped with big wide tracks that kept it on top of the snow.

Tanks and trucks could get through on most of the roads, but it was almost impossible to use a Jeep and a trailer full of supplies. The weasel made our job much easier.

When our guys jumped off on an attack, they fought their way across fields and through the woods, often times in snow up to their butts. Evitts and I loaded the weasel with ammo and rations and followed them across country. We didn't worry about them getting lost – even without the tracks in the snow there was always a trail of dead Krauts that was easy to follow.

During the Battle of the Bulge, there was the Molmedy Massacre. More than a hundred American G.I.s were captured and herded into an open field where they were killed by machine gun fire. Although this was probably one of the minor atrocities of the many war crimes committed by the Nazis, I do hope that the Kraut pigs responsible will fry in Hell forever!

Somewhere along the way, I came down with a bad cold and the hershey squirts caught up with me. One big cough came on so quick I didn't have time to tighten up the pucker string, and what a mess! I had to strip from the waist down and try to wash myself clean with snow. It was miserable, but I was fortunate to have some clean long johns and socks to put on. From that day on, I was a real stinker, because I could smell myself coming and going.

From day one, the weather during the Battle of the Bulge had been against us. The snow and cold were bad enough, but the cloudy sky and the fog made it even worse. We needed air support. We prayed and hoped and then our prayers were answered. There were the sun and the blue sky and the planes.

We were high on a ridge overlooking a valley, and we could see a train coming our way. Of course, I never knew whether it was a supply train or a troop train, but I have always hoped it was filled with Krauts. Each time a plane made a pass, the pilot fired his machine guns and released a couple of rockets. What a beautiful sight! In about two minutes that train was rubble, on fire from one end to the other.

I remember the day a convoy of trucks brought us a re-supply of ammo and rations. We were carrying cases and cartons from the trucks and piling them in the ditch. There was a narrow gauge railroad track on the shoulder of the road, and on one of my trips back and forth, I stepped on the track. When I slipped and fell, the case of 60-mm mortar ammo I was carrying came down on my knee. The combat pants we were wearing were big and roomy, but in a few minutes I had slit the leg to relieve the pressure on my swollen knee. I was sure the kneecap was broken but after a couple of weeks in the hospital I was walking again.

I never did know where we were, so the following is from my "History of the 508th P.I.R.:

On January 11, we had been relieved and were in a rest area close to Chevron, Belgium.

On January 21 we moved to the Deidenberg area. There was little activity there, so once again we moved on January 26 to the front near St. Vith.

Holzheiro was taken by the 1st Battalion and Medendorf was secured by the 2nd Battalion.

On February 20, the 508th went back to Sissonne, and this time it was tents again. There was more training with new replacements, and then in April we packed our bags again. They herded us into forty and eights in Laon and we went to an airfield at Chartres, a short distance from Paris. As soon as we were settled in they brought up a full combat load of ammo to be rolled into bundles that would be dropped with us when we jumped.

This time we were not sealed in as we had been before, and to some extent, the tension of waiting for another combat jump was eased by passes into Paris. When they brought us another full combat load of ammo we began to wonder what in hell is going on.

Time went by and nothing happened, and finally on May 7 we learned that the war in Europe was over. Apparently, it had been anticipated the end was near.

We were at the airfield with a double load of ammo because of the possibility there might be some pockets of continued resistance or the Krauts might begin slaughtering the G.I.s in the P.O.W. camps. If that had happened, we could have been scattered around, a company here and a battalion there. But it didn't happen, and now the war was over and now we could go home!

That was what we thought, but it didn't work that way. Believe it or not, we were told there wasn't one outfit in the European theater that wanted to go home. They were all hoping to be chosen for the highest honor that could be bestowed — honor guard at General Eisenhower's headquarters.

From a military point of view, it was undoubtedly an honor because the assignment would be made in recognition of the elite, the sharpest outfit in the E.T.O. But from a personal point of view, it simply meant another six months overseas on occupation duty. I kept my hopes up, but it didn't help.

14

Most of our journey to Frankfurt was by rail, in the good old forty and eights and along the way we saw the results of the bombs. I remember one area in Cologne that had been leveled — for almost as far as we could see, the only thing standing was one lone chimney. It was a beautiful sight, lovely to behold.

The last leg of our trip was in a truck convoy, and we arrived in Frankfurt on June 10, 1945. There was a lot of rubble in Frankfurt, but the thing I remember best is the welcome we received. The streets were lined with Krauts waving American flags and cheering, and more Krauts were waving American flags from windows. There didn't seem to be even one Nazi left.

The apartments we moved into were in Heddernheim, a suburb of Frankfurt. The Krauts living there were evicted. They were given notice to pack their personal belongings and leave, and there was no coming back for another load. It was block after block of small identical apartments, each with a living room and kitchen down, two bedrooms and a bath up. The Krauts were allowed to take with them only clothing and bedding, so when we moved in, the apartments were completely furnished – electric stove, refrigerator, hot water heater, and furniture.

The mess sergeant and the supply sergeant are always good buddies, so when he needed something from the supply room, he got it, and my refrig. was well stocked. My assistant in the supply room was an excellent cook, so we dined high on the hog, and life was very comfortable. Comfortable but not good, be-

cause there is no way to have a good life in the army
when you are a civilian in uniform waiting to go home.

I am thankful I was excused from all formations,
all drills, all parades, and guard duty. As I recall, the
guard duty wasn't too bad. I think it was eight hours
on and forty hours off, which usually left plenty of time
for baseball, softball, football or passes into town. Of
course, there were company formations for calisthenics or a two- or three-mile double time Ho! And then
there were the parades.

It was to be expected there would be many important people visiting General Eisenhower's E. T. O.
Headquarters. When President Truman arrived he had
to review the troops and there was a parade. When
Secretary of War Stimson arrived, he had to review
the troops and there was a parade. When Under Secretary of War Patterson visited us, he had to review
the troops and there was a parade. When Marshall
Zhukov arrived, there was a parade. When Prince
Bernard of the Netherlands arrived there was a parade. And so it went, on and on. There also was a
parade when Sonja Heine arrived.

As I think back, I remember I did have a little
guard duty because in Frankfurt we were garrison
troops and there was no liquor ration for the lowly G.I.
We had a company party once a month and when it
was your turn, you better damn well have enough booze
for a battalion because some of those guys could smell
a party a mile away. I was responsible for the gathering of the booze and this was no problem. Besides
being a good cook, my assistant was first class
scrounger, so I put him in charge of the Liquor Pro-

curement Detail. Whenever he returned to the company, the Jeep was full of Cognac, brandy, whiskey, beer, and wine. My guard duty was to be sure none of it disappeared before party time.

One of the first orders was there would be no fraternization with the Krauts. There was really no reason to go into Frankfurt because there was little there but rubble and trouble. It was safe to go in the daylight if you were with two or three buddies. At night it was probably almost as dangerous as strolling through Grant Park in Chicago.

If you wanted to gamble a little, there was usually some action in one of the apartments — either craps or poker. One night about 2 A.M., someone was pounding on the door of the supply room. When I went down, DeSimone said, "Drake, you got any money?" I said, "Yes." And he said, "Give me all you got. I'm out almost $2,000 and I can't quit now." I gave him $800 and he said, "I'll pay you back tomorrow." The next morning, he not only paid me, he gave me double! DeSimone was a good buddy, but he was also one of the good reasons I didn't play craps or poker.

There was a point system set up for eligibility for discharge. I don't remember the details, but it was like points for months of service, months overseas, battle stars, medals, etc. For many of us, the duty in Frankfurt was mostly a matter of marking off each day on the calendar. They were literally begging us to stay in Frankfurt so we could go home with the outfit and be in a big parade in New York City. If there was one thing we didn't need, it was another parade.

It seemed to take forever, but when I finally met

the quota for points, I packed my duffel bag and headed for Berlin, the first leg of my journey home. The 82nd had been assigned to occupation duty in Berlin, and I was to head home with a bunch of their guys.

For some reason there had not been much of a black market in Frankfurt. We did some bartering with a carton of cigarettes or some candy bars, like for maybe a camera or some booze, but that was about it. In Berlin it had apparently been a different story, and when I arrived there the stories I heard were almost unbelievable! A pound of used coffee grounds was good for $100. Any old fountain pen that was still working would bring at least $1,000. A watch that was ticking would bring a minimum of $5,000. It was an automatic court martial for anyone who had been issued a G.I. watch and didn't have it in his possession. The market was also good for shirts, pants, boots or whatever.

All this was something else. But hear this! All of our troops in Germany were paid in what was called "occupation" money. It was issued in Kraut Mark denominations and we could spend it there or get a money order and send it home in good old American bucks. If you went on pass, and peddled a few items, and came back to camp with $5,000 in German Marks, you didn't have to sit on it for very long. The next morning you sent home a money order for $5,000 American bucks. This had gone on for months before someone finally wised up to what was going on. When I arrived in Berlin, the good old days were gone — it was a money order once a month for your pay plus 10 percent.

When I was assigned to a company in the 82nd, and when the company commander learned I was a supply sergeant, he didn't order me to report to him; he came to see me and when he told me he had a problem he wasn't kidding.

Although the company supply sergeant was responsible for keeping records for all equipment received and issued, the ultimate responsibility was on the company commander. Usually, if a G.I. lost a piece of equipment, it was replaced but it had to be paid for on a "statement of charges." The company commander was personally responsible when an inventory showed there was equipment missing in the supply room.

I went to the supply room, and it looked like someone had had a garage sale. Along with the other supplies, there were even some rifles missing. I tried to check the records, but there were enough to give me any help.

The only exception for responsibility was when we came back from combat, because no one could avoid losing equipment on the line. To make a long story short, I made out the report of missing supplies, and the Captain and I both certified they were lost in combat. The report was approved and the Captain was ahead about $20,000.

15

Finally, at long last, I was on my way home. At the LeHarve port, we boarded a Liberty ship and set sail for New York. For a while, all went well, including the gambling. I don't know what the stakes were at the craps tables, but I can remember watching the poker games. Can you believe seven-card stud at $100 per card?

Then it was announced we were changing course because we were headed for a severe storm. Then it was announced we were changing course again and heading for New York. The end result was that we hit the storm head on.

When they battened down the hatches and we had to go below, that little ship was jumping around like a fart in a hot skillet. We tied ourselves to the narrow bunks to keep from being tossed out onto the floor. They had to cut down the speed of the engines, but even after they did this, every time the back end of the ship went up and the props cleared the water, they revved up until it sounded like the ship was going to shake into pieces.

I was thinking, "After three years fighting, and after we had once again made the world safe for democracy, and now I was finally going home, this would sure be a hell of a time to go!" The one consolation we had was that in December the water in the North Atlantic is so cold that in three minutes we would be numb and feel no pain.

We docked in New York and from there it was on to the Separation Center in Fort Sheridan where I received me discharge papers and my "Ruptured Duck" lapel pin. I was told, "Wherever you go, always wear this pin and you will be recognized and honored as a veteran."

It was a bitter cold day at the train station in Chicago. Many of the old steam engines were frozen and out of commission. After waiting most of the day, I finally caught the only train heading north.

Char met me at the depot in Beloit where she was teaching. On December 24 we were home in Menomonee, and it was a good Christmas.

So ends my tale, and I just lucked out again, because this is the last sheet on my pad.

Printed in the United States
992200001B